"Packed full of practical wisdom, … engagement, this book will grow … younger generations. It is biblica… packed with real-life stories of h… real deal. I know few people who have served in gospel work amongst teenagers so faithfully and in such a diverse range of contexts. Readers will not only 'catch' his distilled wisdom but some of his contagious passion to see a lost generation encounter Jesus."

**PHIL KNOX,** Evangelist, Evangelical Alliance

"This is more than a book—it is a heartfelt call to action, a roadmap for potential revival and a compassionate invitation to rediscover the church's mission to young people. With clarity and conviction, O'Boyle combines robust research, personal testimony and biblical insight to illuminate the spiritual hunger rising among today's youth. This must-read book will stir your heart, challenge your assumptions and launch your ministry into deeper waters."

**DAVE NEWTON,** National Director, Scripture Union England & Wales

"*Catching the Wave* is an honest field guide for churches that want to love Gen Z and Gen Alpha with care and clarity. O'Boyle puts prayer first and then lets the research and practice speak without reduction or hype, offering simple, credible steps any church can try. I commend it to pastors and youth teams who want a shared starting point that is spiritually serious and practically doable. *Catching the Wave* is for those of us who need to swallow our pride, me included, and try what actually works."

**ALANZO JULIAN PAUL,** Speaker and Tutor, The Oxford Centre for Christian Apologetics; Director, Reboot

"This book lands at just the right time. Grounded in real stories, fresh research and Scripture that steadies everything, it will lift your faith and challenge you to join in with what God is already doing among our nation's young people. Read it prayerfully, expectantly. And get ready—not just to ride the wave that Neil describes but to help the church become a place where the next generation doesn't just visit but truly encounters Jesus."

**RACHEL GARDNER,** Director of Partnerships, Youthscape; Youth Innovation Lead, St Luke's Blackburn

"If you are wanting to see young people's lives changed by Jesus in your community and wondering where to begin, then this book is for you. Beautiful in tone and wonderfully practical, it gives insight about a generation alongside a vision of what transformation through Jesus could look like in your community."

**LAURA HANCOCK,** National Ministries Director, British Youth for Christ

"An inspiring and practical introduction from an experienced practitioner on how local churches can catch up with what God is doing with young people."

**STU GIBBS,** Newday Generation

"An essential guide to the challenges and opportunities for churches aiming to engage with Gen Z and Gen Alpha. Neil captures the essence of understanding the worlds these young people inhabit, marked by their unique values and struggles. *Catching the Wave* is a heartfelt call to connect authentically with younger generations and make faith accessible in today's rapidly changing world."

**DAN BLYTHE,** Global Youth Director, Alpha

"What is the faith of the next generation worth to us? It should be everything, right? And after decades of difficult and even depressing news about the church and our nation, it does seem God is doing a 'new' thing. People—especially young people—are arriving at church in search of God. In this book Neil provides a resource and inspiration that is rich in research, story, example and challenge. He calls the church to a season of readiness and a posture of expectancy. Let's catch the wave!"

**LEON EVANS,** Founder, Further Faster Network;
Lead Pastor, Lifecentral Church

"*Catching the Wave* stirs faith, speaks to the real needs of young people and equips the church to respond with both compassion and conviction. A move of God is stirring among Gen Z-A, and this book helps us step into it!"

**SAMMY JABANGWE-HANTON,** Youth Evangelist, The Message Trust

Neil O'Boyle

# Catching the Wave

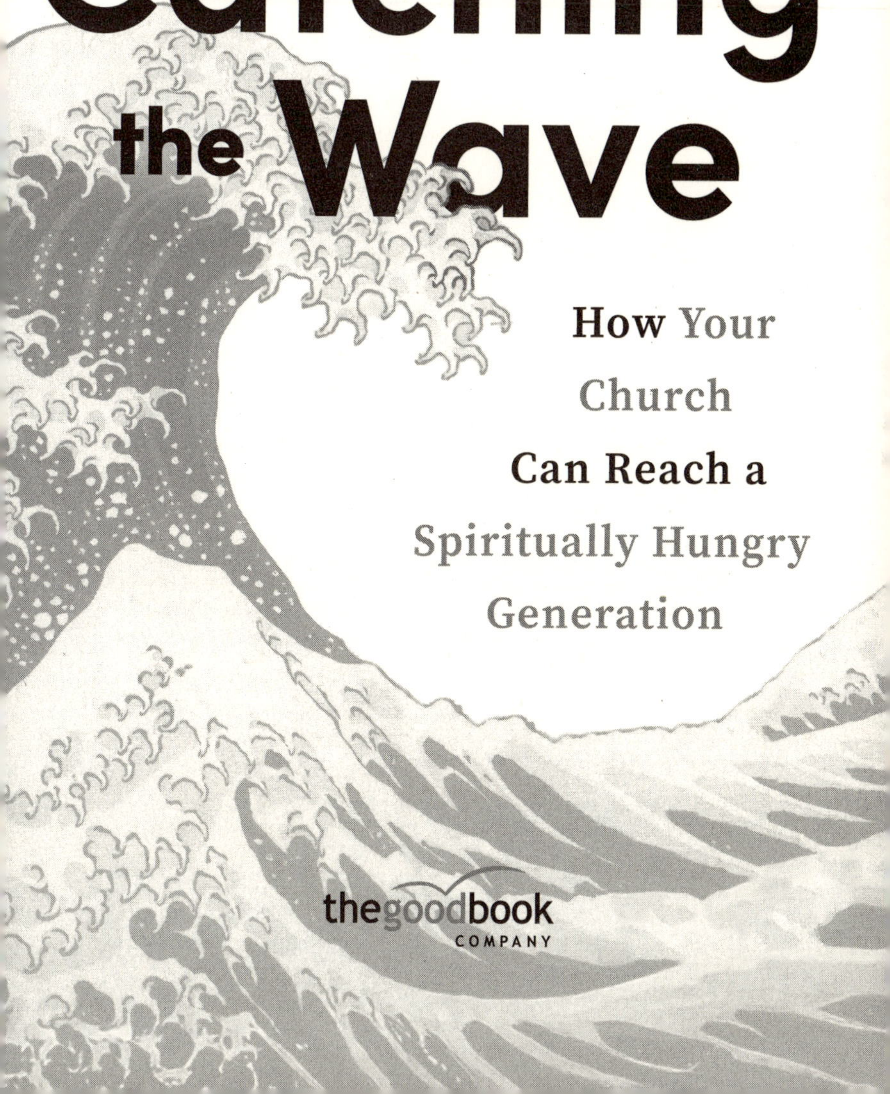

## How Your Church Can Reach a Spiritually Hungry Generation

thegoodbook COMPANY

Catching the Wave



Published by:
The Good Book Company

thegoodbook.com | thegoodbook.co.uk
thegoodbook.com.au | thegoodbook.co.nz



Some names have been changed in the real-life stories in this book.

Every book published by The Good Book Company has been written by a human author and edited by a human editor. While AI tools are sometimes used to assist with research and support certain processes, all content has been created by a human author and thoroughly checked by our editorial team to ensure it is biblically faithful and pastorally wise.



Cover design by Drew McCall

A CIP catalogue record for this book is available from the British Library.

ISBN: 9781802544169 | JOB-008576 | Printed in India

# Contents

# About the Author

**NEIL O'BOYLE HAS** spent more than three decades walking alongside young people and church communities in the UK and around the world. His heart is to see the church live out an invitational and missional culture, where both churched and unchurched young people encounter Jesus in everyday life. As National Director of Youth for Christ Britain, Neil has championed evangelism and discipleship that are rooted in Scripture, Spirit-led and shaped by real cultural understanding.

# Author's Note

**IN THIS BOOK,** you will often see the terms Gen Alpha and Gen Z.

Generation Z refers to those born approximately between 1996 and 2010.

Generation Alpha refers to those born from about 2010 up to the mid-2020s.

Throughout this book, Gen Z and Gen Alpha are often referred to collectively as Gen Z-A or simply as Z-A.

# 1

# Starting Within

Chapter 1

# Ready for Revival

**"WE JUST BAPTISED** three young people this weekend, and there are even more lined up to be baptised in the next few weeks!"

I was visiting Dan, a Youth for Christ staff worker in the north of England. When I arrived, Dan had just wrapped up a meeting with the local pastor, who was buzzing with excitement.

Not long ago, this church had been hanging on by a thread. It had mostly elderly members, a few coffee mornings and a leaky roof. But something had shifted. The church was now growing—and it was growing with young people! Teenagers, to be precise.

Not long before my visit, Dan had run a mission week in the local school and invited pupils to a Friday-night outreach event at the church. There was no flashy band, no smoke machine, no hype. It was a simple event, but something powerful happened. Dozens of young people showed up wanting to know more about Jesus. They specifically wanted to know how to become Christians.

Fast-forward two months, and after conversations with their parents (who weren't churchgoers), these same young people were getting baptised. Others had already joined the church. There was something happening in this community.

And it isn't just Dan's community. There is something happening in this nation: a gentle awakening to faith. It's been documented across a range of demographics but particularly among the young. Every week, stories are bubbling to the surface of teenagers without any faith background simply turning up at churches to discover God.

At the organisation that I have led for the past decade, British Youth for Christ, we weren't satisfied with anecdotal evidence; we wanted to understand the data behind the stories. We commissioned a research company to find out just how spiritually open today's 11-18-year-olds really are. Our report, published in the summer of 2025, was called *Z-A: Growing Spirituality.*

Back in 2020, approximately 4% of young people in the UK were attending church.[1] Five years later, when we asked 11-18-year-olds across Britain, "Is attending church part of your weekly activity?" a staggering 8% said yes.[2] That's double the number from five years ago! Twice as many now attend church. Similarly, in 2020, roughly 52% of young people believed in some kind of spiritual being greater than themselves. That openness has increased; now it is 68%.

From 2020 until now, there has been a 12% rise in young people who identify as followers of Jesus, a 12% rise in those who pray, and a 12% rise in those who pray daily.[3] In 2020, only 8% said they viewed the church positively, but when we asked again in 2025, the dial had shifted considerably; 65% now viewed it positively, though there were still concerns around its institutional authority. What happened in those five years? A pandemic for one, but perhaps a stirring of the Holy Spirit for another.

At around the same time, the Bible Society conducted some similar research called *The Quiet Revival*. This report found that there are over 2 million more people attending church in the UK than there were six years ago. Significantly, the charge is being led by the young; 16% of 18-24-year-olds now attend church at least once a month.[4]

You don't have to be a youth worker to be excited about these statistics. We have an amazing opportunity here! The question is: are we ready for it? There's a wave coming, but will we catch it?

## Running to Welcome

Perhaps one of the most familiar stories in the Gospels is the story of the prodigal son in Luke 15. A young man runs away from his family, rejecting his father and heading off to seek a life of pleasure. Drinking, parties, sleeping around—the works. This boy is a disgrace. But when he finally runs out of money, ending up as an underfed pig-keeper, he decides to go back to his father.

The son is looking for safety and security—a place where life will make sense again. Riddled as he must be with regret and shame, home seems like the only possible source of what he desperately needs. But he goes there without expecting much of a welcome—he knows what he has done. He plans to offer himself as a servant. He knows he's not worthy to be called his father's son.

But what happens? Don't let familiarity rob you of the beauty of this moment!

> *While he was still a long way off, his father saw him and was filled with compassion for him; he ran to his son, threw his arms round him and kissed him.*
>
> *(Luke 15:20)*

The father welcomes his broken son. Not only that—he runs to meet him! This father goes out of his way to find his lost son and welcome him home.

It's a picture of our heavenly Father welcoming those who have (knowingly or unknowingly) turned their back on him and pursued another way, but who are now seeking forgiveness. But it can also be a picture of us. Are we not God's ambassadors here on earth (2 Corinthians 5:20), called to reach the lost, broken, uncertain, disconnected and marginalised?

Young people today are all of those things. Yes, they are starting to come back to church, and it's exciting. But there is still very often a hesitation or even hostility about Christian things. An increasing openness to spirituality comes alongside a distrust of authority and institutions and a perception that the church hates gay people. There are ways in which the very values of society seem at odds with biblical belief. Meanwhile, the sheer distraction of the digital revolution can make it hard for young people to engage with the good news of Jesus.

What's my point? Young people may be coming back to church, but we shouldn't expect them to just slot in easily as if they've always belonged. Nor should we expect every young person to be able to make the first move themselves.

Like the father of the prodigal son, we need to run to meet them!

## Starting the Journey

If you are not seeing unchurched young people engaging with your church, don't panic or feel disillusioned—you still can! In fact, this entire book has been written for those who would like to see more unchurched young people walk through their doors. We're going to talk about lots of different things you can do to reach out to those who have no connection with church yet. This book also provides assistance for those who already have young people in their church but aren't sure how to integrate unchurched young people.

Section 1 calls us to look *within*: what is the situation, and what do we need to ask God to do within us, both as individuals and as the church? At the opposite end of the book, section 4 has the most practical chapters, with a focus on going *out* and finding ways to engage with unchurched young people, whether in schools, in the community or in our church buildings. But before we do that, in sections 2 and 3 we're going to try to understand this generation better. We go *deep*, focusing on what matters to Gen Z and Alpha and how to communicate with them about God. Then we look *wide*, with an exploration of some of the particular struggles and challenges young people are facing, and how we can care for the whole person as we reach out to welcome. It's the wider-angle view that we need before we can get really practical in section 4.

This book is a starting point. It's not a comprehensive guide to every model of youth work or every facet of youth culture. Instead it's designed to help you take the first steps in a journey of sharing Jesus with a generation that desperately needs to hear his good news.

### Are We Ready?

Rodney Gypsy Smith was a famous revivalist in the late 19th and early 20th centuries. He travelled up and down Britain, crossed the Atlantic 45 times (no easy task in those days!) and met with two different presidents at the White House. He preached to millions of people and saw many respond to Jesus. Unsurprisingly, other Christians would come to Smith and say, "How can we have the same revival impact as you do?" But his reply may have been unexpected:

> *Go into an empty room, close the door, draw a circle on the floor with chalk, kneel within that circle and ask God to revive everything inside the circle.*[5]

I want us to take Smith's advice as we begin our journey. Before we look out, we need to look within. Are we individually ready? Furthermore, are we collectively ready? Is your church both hopeful and prepared? What would it take for it to become so?

When Jesus approached Simon and Andrew, who were fishing on the lake, he called out to them to follow him. Because we know the story well, we may breeze past it—but their decision to drop everything and obey Jesus' call is rather dramatic when you think about it. Did Jesus' reputation precede him? Was his personality so infectious that one felt compelled to comply with his requests? We don't know. What we do know, however, is that the fishermen acted on the invitation. So when Jesus said, "Come, follow me ... and I will send you out to fish for people" (Matthew 4:19), Simon and Andrew said yes! They were all in!

We, too, can be fishers of people—we can see our nets fill to excess as young people turn to Jesus in their droves. It all starts by simply saying "Yes" to Jesus' call.

Chapter 2

# Making the Effort

**"HE'S NOT MY** God!" shouted the teenage girl on a packed train.

She had my attention; I was fixated on the heated discussion taking place behind me as the girl's friends mocked her: "Yes he is! You believe in God!"

"No, I don't!" she replied.

But they were unrelenting. "Yes you do—why are you denying it? You go to church, we know you do!" Their laughs and comments were unflattering.

At last she admitted it. "Yeah, okay, I do believe in God! So what?"

"Only stupid people believe in God today!" the others scoffed.

There was so much I took from that conversation. It was only a few days after we'd got our research back at Youth for Christ. I had been so excited to learn that belief is up and around a third of all young people in the UK want someone to tell them about God. But to imply that there is a complete softening and receptivity to God among young people would be misleading. The door to spirituality has swung open, and there is a stirring—a wave of the Holy Spirit. But it isn't straightforward. In this chapter, we're going to look in a bit more detail at why that is.

### A Complex View of Church

"Boring."

"Don't get it."

"Toxic."

"Misogynistic."

"Hateful."

"Judgmental."

These are just a few of the responses young people give when asked about church. While Z-A is generally positive towards churches and most believe they would be welcomed, there are still significant negative stigmas to get past.

When Gen Z was asked why they don't turn to religion in tough times, 60% said they didn't agree with aspects of what religious groups were teaching, 58% wanted to figure out faith for themselves instead of having it handed to them, and 56% felt they didn't need a faith community—they could find meaning elsewhere.[6]

In other words, today's teens don't agree with the church on issues of lifestyle, don't want a construct of someone else's faith, and don't need a faith community to find meaning and connection. On the one hand, there is a rise in church attendance among Gen Z, yet on the other, an overwhelming uncertainty about whether religion and a religious community are the answer.

This isn't a simple "we love church" or "we dislike it", but rather a complex, mushed-up bundle of thoughts. While some with no church background are certainly turning up to church, the majority are not, and nor are they likely to. Therefore, the burden rests with the church community as to whether we wish to engage with this spiritually hungry generation of young people.

In the 1990s, an indestructible bridge was built in Honduras, a nation hit frequently by aggressive weather conditions. Using state-of-the-art infrastructure and Japanese technology, the Choluteca Bridge was designed to withstand a hurricane. Within the very year the bridge was opened, Hurricane Mitch swept through Honduras, destroying anything in its way. With the exception of the bridge. As per its design, it endured very little damage; however, the roads on either side were completely demolished and disappeared. Meanwhile, the hurricane had been so aggressive that it physically altered the flow of the river, which no longer passed under the bridge. The Choluteca Bridge stood alone, with no road connections and without even a river underneath it. It was now known as the bridge to nowhere.

From the perspective of many young people, the church, too, seems like a bridge to nowhere. It stands alone; its days might appear to have come and gone. Young people are seeking other ways to "cross the river"—to find guidance, answers or solutions to life's problems. Take WitchTok, the collective name for witchcraft-related videos on the social media platform TikTok, which is proving to be a major attraction for young females seeking to connect spirituality with feminism.[7] WitchTok videos had gained 64.8 billion views by mid-2024.[8] Meanwhile, in the States, research shows that young people are more likely to feel connected to nature than to a higher power.[9] These are just two of many examples.

Here's the reality: the good news of Jesus is seen as only one option in a whole host of competing spiritualities. And it may well not seem the most appealing of those options.

## Something Is Broken

When something is broken on a car or machine, we often know because of the noise it makes. It might clang, bang or crackle, but whatever the sound, it's certainly not the same gentle hum it gives off when all is well.

Such a noise surrounds Gen Z-A today—and this is the second reason I want to highlight as to why welcoming young people into church is not necessarily straightforward. Here are six news headlines from just one month in 2024 that show how dramatic things can get.

> *Pupil behaviour "getting worse" at schools in England, say teachers: Nearly one in five teachers in England has been hit by a pupil this year, a survey commissioned by the BBC says*[10]

> *What is really going on with Gen Alpha boys ... Inquiry into the rise of misogamy among boys and young men*[11]

*Suicide is on the rise for young Americans, with no clear answers*[12]

*Children as young as 13 sold knives and blades in police sting operation*[13]

*Girl arrested on suspicion of attempted murder after teachers and pupil stabbed at school*[14]

*England child alcohol use tops global charts, finds WHO report*[15]

Of course, these headlines only show part of the story. Positive news doesn't always make the front page. Yet it's clear that something is significantly broken when it comes to today's generation. Violence, misogyny, underage drinking... What has gone wrong?

All of this profoundly bothers me. I am not comfortable knowing how troubled many young people are and how much they need love, acceptance and care. I long for youth outreach to receive the focus and attention it needs. I fear that, too often, we just don't care enough.

## Scum and Scorn

In Jesus' day, there were plenty of broken, troublesome and dysfunctional people around. According to the religious leaders of the time, they polluted society and went against the laws of the Torah. We can see their attitude in Luke 5:30, where the Pharisees and teachers of the law complain about the people attending a huge party held in Jesus' honour. "Why do you eat and drink with tax collectors and sinners?"

they ask in disgust. For the Pharisees, these people are scum. They aren't religious, don't act in accordance with the teachings of Scripture and have little to no respect for religious law.

But Jesus responds:

> *It is not the healthy who need a doctor, but those who are ill. I have not come to call the righteous, but sinners to repentance. (Luke 5:31-32)*

The passage has my mind racing. How likely is it that in today's society, young people could be looked at with similar judgments? How often have you heard that today's young people are troubled, wayward, misguided, lazy, opinionated and digitally addicted? That they lack social integration and have questionable values? Aren't these the same things (with the exception of digital addiction) that could have been said about tax collectors?

This comparison leads to a challenging question: if today's teens are the tax collectors, what is their experience or expectation of today's Pharisee equivalents—those who are established, well educated, affluent and religious?

Many teens are not hearing the radical welcome of Jesus—the gospel call to repentance and faith. Instead they hear the church's message as one of judgment.

There is a concern among Gen Z and Gen Alpha that the church lacks authenticity and is judgmental of people's lifestyles. Of the young people in our *Z-A: Growing Spirituality* research who did not feel they would be welcomed at church, many of those assumed they would be unwelcome due to lifestyle preferences; others thought it would be over the fact that they didn't believe.[16] That's a sobering reality. The ranking by young people in the report placed the church a fraction above the government, which is often seen as just another institution to distrust.

It's true that Christians' views on certain issues clash with modern secular expectations. The Bible has messages that today's young people may not want to hear, on everything from sexuality to identity to sin. But there was a clash between the tax collectors' lifestyle and the biblical commands too—and it didn't stop Jesus from talking to them.

The question for us is: do we write young people off in the same way the Pharisees wrote off the tax collectors? Perhaps we don't actively dismiss them, but we do remain apathetic, letting them assume the worst of us. Do we leave them in their broken, abandoned, sin-stained state? Or do we reach out, as Jesus did, and invite them in?

Seeking to be relevant and effective in our witness to young people does *not* mean we need to deconstruct our faith and throw out the authority of Scripture. Just as Jesus did not hesitate to tell the tax collectors that there is a better way, so we need to stick to our commitment to demonstrate and declare Jesus and his gospel—the whole gospel, with its call to die to self and follow God's ways.

Yet we need to look at that gospel truth through a different lens. We need to be aware of the noise caused by brokenness—the harmful influences, broken relationships and deep confusion that so many young people are experiencing. We need to care enough to make the effort to consider how we can meet young people where they are, how we will come across to them and how we can help them experience a taste of life as it's really meant to be.

I am reminded often of Jesus' words in John 10:10: "The thief comes only to steal and kill and destroy". Truly, the enemy is killing, stealing and destroying in our own day. But Jesus went on, "I have come that they may have life, and have it to the full."

The mission is clear; the how becomes our challenge.

**We Need the Holy Spirit**

In the spring of 2024, I was late for the youth leaders' pre-meeting. One young person had already arrived: a 13-year-old boy whom I knew well—I had spent lots of time with him, helping to address major bullying in his life. I quickly asked, "You okay?" and he raised his eyebrows with a smile. He was tucking into a well-known brand of fast food. I apologised for not chatting but said I would be back out in ten minutes or so.

After the meeting, I found the boy slumped. Something had happened. "You okay?" I asked again, with a greater degree of clarity than before. The answer was no. In the brief time I had been in the meeting, the boy had received news that one of his friends, a 13-year-old girl, had overdosed and taken her own life. I sat, listened and said very little while he told me the story. He concluded by saying, "We shouldn't have to deal with this stuff."

What disturbed me the most that day? Perhaps surprisingly, it wasn't the tragic death of a 13-year-old girl who had lost hope. Nor was it the boy overwhelmed by pain and confusion. It was my own reaction. To my shame, I was barely moved.

I understood why. When you work with hurting and vulnerable young people, challenges often follow. This wasn't the first teen suicide I had known, and I am sadly convinced it won't be the last. One of my own daughters has lost three friends (all teenagers) to suicide. That's three funerals, three devastated families and three young people who just couldn't cope. I was becoming immune, desensitised, hardened—whatever label you want to give it—to that which is unthinkable: a young person ending their life.

I went home and prayed that God would break my heart, remove the callouses, and help me do all I can to fight for a generation facing sizeable challenges and changes that no previous generation can fully understand or identify with. A generation hearing a thousand competing messages that seem so easily to drown out the good news they could encounter in Jesus.

I want to encourage you to ask the Holy Spirit to examine your heart as you read through this book. To point out areas that may be hardened, or where biases have formed that may not be in line with Jesus, or where apathy has taken hold. The Holy Spirit does not condemn, but he will convict—and that conviction can transform us.

This book will help with the next steps, but permission and willingness for the heart's examination are entirely with you and the Holy Spirit. To catch and be part of the wave moving through this nation, there can be only one starting place, and that is prayer—as we will explore over the following pages.

Chapter 3

# We Go Slow

**HOPEFULLY, YOU HAVE** a sense of purpose beginning to bubble up—a conviction that your church should engage with unchurched young people. So now what?

It's time to push into what God might be asking you to do. There are so many possibilities—so many great ways to engage with today's teens. As we go through the pages of this book, you will pick up lots of ideas through the stories and examples I share. However, before we rush ahead, I want to make a suggestion.

"We go slow, we go together!"

The guide instructed my team with those words at the very bottom of Mount Kilimanjaro. We would ascend Africa's largest mountain, just over 19,000 feet high, in roughly three days. Slow didn't feel like a good option. In fact, I was sent to the back of our single-file group numerous times for trying to speed up our guide.

Everything about me struggles with patience. If I am going somewhere, I want to get there, and if there is a problem, I want to fix it. So I understand how you might be feeling right now. While the number of young people attending church has doubled, there is still an extremely long way to go. The vast majority of young people in the UK have no regular connection with church. It is tempting, then, either to skip ahead to the chapters where the "fix" can be found or to disengage because it's all a bit of a mountain to climb.

But I want to encourage you to go slow: read each chapter at a pace that allows you to absorb and reflect. If you do feel overwhelmed, there is so much to follow that will encourage you. If you decide to skip forward and just get to the "how", then you will miss out on some very important pieces along the way—such as this chapter, which is key to the entire book.

The biggest reason for wanting you to slow down can be found at the very point the global church first accelerated. That might seem contradictory. How can slowing down and accelerating occur simultaneously?

### The Birth of the Church

> *[The believers] devoted themselves to the apostles' teaching and to fellowship, to the breaking of bread and to prayer. (Acts 2:42)*

This verse comes towards the end of an amazing chapter. We are in the days after Jesus has returned to heaven. The Holy Spirit has been poured out on his small band of followers in a dramatic way. Thousands of ordinary folk in Jerusalem have accepted the message of Jesus and have been baptised. Yet the early church resisted the temptation to only do evangelism and perform miracles. They did do that—but they also grounded themselves in receiving teaching, sharpening each other in fellowship, remembering what Jesus had done for them and praying! And look at the result:

> *The Lord added to their number daily those who were being saved. (v 47)*

These early Christians paused, learned and prayed, and people came to faith!

I want to encourage you to ground yourself in good teaching, fellowship and prayer. Particularly in praying together. Not token prayer but real, deliberate prayer, as if the very survival of your community depends on it. Because in many ways it does!

It was around 11 p.m. when I was woken for the final push to the summit of Kilimanjaro. I'd heard that everything up to this point had been easy compared to what lay ahead—and the rumours didn't lie. We gathered around the main tent, wrapped up our water bottles to stop them freezing, and checked gear and oxygen levels. Then we started the final ascent in single file.

By 1 a.m., the temperature had dropped well below zero. Torches began to fade, boots weren't holding up, and our guide used a pickaxe to clear the path. Around 2 a.m., we stopped for a break. Some of the team were suffering—vomiting, hallucinating, frost nip. One guy's socks were soaked with blood. I was doing okay, all things considered. I was rummaging through my bag when, without warning, the team moved on. Panicking, I hurried to catch up—a mistake. We had been told to go slow and go together.

After about 20 minutes, I became aware that everyone was speaking French. Why French? Our team was British. That's when I realised: this team had passed us while we were resting, and I had confused them for my own group. I stopped, unsure of what to do, and watched the French team disappear into the darkness. Now I was alone, on Kilimanjaro, in -20°C windchill. I shouted. Nothing. I was cold, the frost nip setting in. I shouted again.

Then, a faint voice in the distance—our guide: "Stay where you are. Do not move. We are coming!" About 15 minutes later, the group reached me. The guide was furious. I was sent to the back and firmly reminded, "We go slow, and we go together!"

We were the last group to summit—but from what we heard, we were the only team to get every single person to the top. We went slow, and we went together.

As I reflect on that time, I am reminded of a verse from Isaiah:

> *Whether you turn to the right or to the left, your ears will hear a voice behind you, saying, "This is the way; walk in it." (Isaiah 30:21)*

That night, lost on the side of a mountain, I heard a voice behind me—the reassuring voice of the guide. Throughout my 30 years of ministry, I have come to trust that when I feel lost and uncertain and the path is unclear, I need to fight every instinct within me to rush on ahead. I need to settle down and listen, and in time, I will hear the gentle voice of God: "This is the way; walk in it!"

The end goal is mission-critical. But we have to go slow, and we have to go together. We need to plan, and most importantly, we need to pray.

## Pausing to Pray

Often our default way of praying about things is simply to write them down in a list and then ask God for wisdom. That's fine, but there are other ways to pray that you might find helpful as you seek to sense God's direction together.

Below are five suggestions on how you might be able to listen and discern. Before you put any of them into practice, remember that it's really important to test whatever comes to mind in light of Scripture (1 Thessalonians 5:19-22). When we ask God to speak to us, he often does, but sometimes our thoughts just come from our own active imaginations! Before proceeding, ask these questions: What makes me think this is God speaking? How do others respond to what I am sharing? What sense of confirmation can be found in Scripture? When I gently push on doors, are they moving?

### QUIET EXPECTATION

Find a quiet, tidy space. If desired, light a candle to help focus your attention. Invite God to speak to you by saying, "Speak, Lord, for your servant is listening"—it might be helpful to repeat it over and over. Ask God to show you what he would like you to do. Then wait in silence and allow your mind to take you wherever God guides it. Keep a Bible beside you in case verses come to mind. Write down what comes to you. If you're in a group, discuss it. What might it mean (if anything)? Could any of these thoughts be from God?

**PRAYING OVER A MAP**

Place a map of where you live on the floor. Thank God for this community, and ask for God's will to be done for the young people in the area. Ask him to show you something of significance from the map. Then sit in silence and, as you look over the map, allow your mind to go to the things of interest. Write them down and then discuss them with others.

**PRAYER WALKING**

Walk around the neighbourhood. As you walk, praise God for his sovereignty and ask him to destroy anything that is of the enemy within the area, bringing his kingdom rule here instead. You might find it helpful to read Joshua 6:1-27 first. Ask God to bless the young people in the community and pray about any challenges associated with that. Invite God to reveal points of interest or divine opportunities as you walk. Afterwards, discuss with others what grabbed your attention. Did anything stir you with excitement? Did you notice a need that you might consider addressing?

**SURVEY AND PRAYER**

Walk around the neighbourhood, but this time stop and talk to people, explaining that you are from the church and you are praying for the local area. What would they like you to ask God to do for this community? After you have collected some feedback, bring it back to the group to pray together about it. There will be things people said that may be far-fetched or outside of what you may be able to offer. But some tangible things may have been mentioned that the church could provide. Or perhaps you notice that the area would benefit from something that is currently outside of your resources but could be a real game-changer. Don't dismiss it. Pray into it.

**WORDS OF SIGNIFICANCE**

Prepare 26 index cards, each labelled with a letter from A to Z. For each letter, think of a name, place or activity related to young people in your context—e.g. A for "A-Level Students", B for "Bike Club", C for "Community Centre". If you can't think of something, cross out that letter—those are your blank cards. Shuffle and hand out the cards face down. In pairs or as a group, pray for what's on your card. If you get a blank, set it aside and pick one with a word. Ask God to show you its importance and if there's anything you should do. After praying, return to the blank cards. Sit in silence and ask God if there's anything else he wants to show you—then write it down. Finally, discuss each card. Rate its significance—high, medium, or low—and share any thoughts or insights. What might God be saying?

It may well be that the clarity you need on what to do next does not come until you have finished this book. Note what stories, practical suggestions and Bible references you are particularly drawn to as you read. Consider how you feel about these ideas (does this fill you with dread or excite you?), and then take time to examine the practical side (do you have the resources and people you need at the times you would need them?), and consider what opportunities are already available to you.

Remember, don't rush this process. It is better to minister in the right areas but do it slowly, rather than jumping in where you aren't being called to (just yet at least).

### The Rewards of Persistence

I was curious about one of the largest local youth ministries I have seen in some time. Over 400 people attended an event I was asked to speak at. What was their secret? What had they done to foster such growth? How come they were so successful?

The answer was prayer!

I nodded but asked about their methods of engagement with young people. I wanted to understand their attractional models. The leaders understood where I was going with my questioning, but they brought it back again to prayer. I was told that years before, the church had had no young people—not a single one! Three dissatisfied members of the congregation met to pray each week for the young people in the community. An entire year passed, and there was no evidence of any young people in church. They continued: one year turned into two, and two years turned into five. Still no young people. They kept praying! Five years remarkably turned into ten! Now, you've got to wonder at what point you start to say, "This isn't working—God obviously has other plans!" They didn't; they kept meeting each week for 20 years.

Finally, one single young person showed up and then another and another. Now they have many.

It reminds me of a story Jesus told:

*In a certain town there was a judge who neither feared God nor cared what people thought. And there was a widow in that town who kept coming to him with the plea, "Grant me justice against my adversary."*

*For some time he refused. But finally he said to himself, "Even though I don't fear God or care what people think, yet because this widow keeps bothering me, I will see that she gets justice, so that she won't eventually come and attack me!" (Luke 18:2-5)*

The persistent widow was fixated on getting what she believed to be right. She wasn't put off by pushback or being ignored. She kept knocking on the judge's door until she got what she deserved: justice!

Jesus told this story to show that we "should always pray and not give up" (v 1). God is far more generous than this grumpy judge. Won't he give us the good things we long for if they are in his will? And we can be sure that young people discovering Jesus is a good thing!

*But do not forget this one thing, dear friends:*
*with the Lord a day is like a thousand years, and a thousand years are like a day. The Lord is not slow in keeping his promise, as some understand slowness. Instead he is patient with you, not wanting anyone to perish, but everyone to come to repentance.*

*(2 Peter 3:8-9)*

What I consider quick and what God considers quick may not always seem to match up. However, I didn't create time, so I am not the authority on what is quick and what is slow. I must defer to the one who did. What matters is not how long something takes (though waiting can be very painful); what matters is the end result!

**When God Speaks**

After the pandemic, Youth for Christ was out of shape. Our pre-pandemic model of ministry no longer worked. Young people had changed. Receptivity had shifted. We were busy but not fruitful. At the same time, funding from trusts and major donors dried up—we were in real financial trouble.

The day I told staff we were considering redundancies, I also said goodbye to a key leader. It hurt. Driving home in silence, I said, "God, this isn't working. I'm not the one to lead anymore."

As I pulled into my drive, a message came through from a friend: "I have a serious word from God for you—call me." I didn't want to, but I trusted the person. I made the call.

"God says Youth for Christ is crumbling," I was told. (This person knew nothing of our situation.) "You can stop, pray and fast for 40 days—if you do, there'll still be crumbling, but his Spirit will move. Or you can keep going—and the crumbling will become unmanageable."

Four days later, we stopped everything, pulled our teams off the road and prayed for 40 days. Two things emerged: first, a reminder that God wanted our hearts, not our professionalism; and second, a clear call to love the local—shifting from large events to a new focus on empowering local churches and centres to reach unchurched young people.

We were like climbers, lost in the dark of the night on the side of a mountain, with God gently whispering, "We go slow, we go together". Or "This is the way—walk in it".

For 30 months, we rebuilt. The mission is unchanged—we want unchurched young people to know Jesus. But the strategy is different: we believe the local church is God's chosen vehicle, and we are called to serve it.

That's you!

I can't overemphasise the importance of prayer if we want to see unchurched young people come to know Jesus and be discipled in the church. In the listening comes clarity of direction. It is so easy to be busy but not fruitful. You are called to be fruitful, but without prayer, you may end up just being busy.

Going slow doesn't mean not going at all. It means getting everything in place so that you can reach the summit. Despite the temptation to rush into action, let me encourage you to pray—and keep praying until you and others start to sense what God might be saying regarding the path he has for you.

> *Ask and it will be given to you; seek and you will find; knock and the door will be opened to you. For everyone who asks receives; the one who seeks finds; and to the one who knocks, the door will be opened.*
>
> *(Luke 11:9-10)*

In the next section we will continue our journey of discernment by understanding who Gen Z-A are, what they care about, and why the gospel of Jesus is such vitally good news for them.

# 2

# Going Deep

Chapter 4

# Gen Z-A and Family

**WE KNOW THAT** young people are spiritually hungry; we know that they desperately need the gospel. But to older generations, today's young people might seem to speak an entirely different language! In a way that's true—Gen Z-A see the world through a different lens. What we need to do is understand what that lens is.

In this section we're going to look at three aspects of Gen Z-A's "lens". For each one, we'll see how this shows us a key starting point for sharing good news—and think about how we can go about communicating that. The first is family and the concept of belonging.

It won't surprise you that surveys have shown that the greatest influence on young people—both in matters of faith and in other areas—is their family.[17] However, everything about family is changing at a rapid rate. To many of us, "family" means two parents, up to four grandparents, and a few siblings—maybe some aunts, uncles and cousins as well. But very sadly, for a great many young people today, family is far, far more complicated than that.

Not long ago I was speaking at a week-long event where I noticed two young people—siblings in their teens—who seemed very much to be on the margins. They didn't get involved in any of the activities but sat alone. They kept themselves entertained but didn't seem very happy. I heard rumblings that they wanted to leave. My focus moved to them. In every break I went over to them to play cards or do whatever else they wanted. They decided to stick around, and over time they began to open up, becoming increasingly chatty.

Gradually the siblings' story came out. Their mum had left their dad due to his abusiveness and excessive drinking. The children had gone with their mum. Even knowing what they knew about him, they still missed their dad, who (from what I could tell) did not seem overly interested in them. But here was the really sticky part for these teenagers: their mum now had a boyfriend. I gathered that although the mum was in her mid-40s, the boyfriend was just a few years older than the oldest sibling. Furthermore he was often in the house, being overly affectionate with their mum in front of the children, and telling them all how to behave.

It made sense that these teenagers were sitting alone at this event. How could they relate to the other participants or explain their home situation? They were in a heap of pain.

Is this unusual? It all depends on what you are comparing it to.

## A Need to Belong

In 1960, only 2% of couples in Britain lived together before marriage, but by 1998 that number had jumped to 75%. By 2008, 40% of marriages were remarriages, and stepfamilies were becoming more common.[18] Today, 17.7% of families are cohabiting couples, and 16.1% are lone-parent families (mostly led by single mothers).[19] Blended families (where each member of a couple brings children from a previous relationship) now make up about one-third of all families in England and Wales.[20] These are huge societal shifts in behaviour and attitudes.

The reality is that humans crave relational security, and children and young people look for that within the family home. When young people are spending a large proportion of their social time on a screen, and with 42% of marriages ending in divorce, there are two major challenges colliding at the same time: loneliness and the instability of family change.

Research shows that children generally do better emotionally, mentally and academically when raised by two married parents. They're less likely to face legal trouble, teen pregnancy, and mental health issues.[21] Secure attachments developed through consistent parental relationships prove to have a profound impact on the wellbeing of young people.[22] A stable home with both parents present makes a difference! Yet for many young people, this is not their reality.

It isn't hard to see how the good news of Jesus fits into this. Gen Z-A may come from a place of broken families, but Jesus came to welcome broken people into God's family. We cannot fix every fallout from a broken home; but it really does make an extraordinary difference when Gen Z-A see that Jesus offers them a place to truly belong.

**God's Family**

Debbie was a single mum, and her situation was complex. She lived in an area of social housing which sat in a tiny corner of a very affluent community. She had two children—Billy, aged 14, and Louise, aged 12—who showed all the signs of deep scarring from the family breakdown.

Debbie could barely pay the bills and did not have enough to eat. When someone is knocking on the door of a church asking if there is any food, that tells you things are extremely tough! Now that she was on the church's radar, however, support was on offer. In response, Debbie felt obliged to attend services (though she wasn't pressured to do so). Fortunately she not only liked them but felt valued in the church.

Billy and Louise, however, did not feel so valued. They joined my youth group—it was my first ever paid ministry job. Socially they felt at a disadvantage. They were economically challenged, while everyone else was from wealthy homes. Their clothes had holes and were often dirty with various stains; their peers in the group wore the latest and the best. Their dad was in and out of prison, whereas most dads in the church were thriving business leaders. Billy and Louise both had learning challenges in a struggling local school. Many of the other young people were privately educated or had private after-school tutoring.

Unsurprisingly, Billy and Louise acted up. They would start fights. I could identify with them; I had been raised in a similar economic background and found the middle-class nature of this church overwhelming. Billy and Louise needed one-on-one care and connection, so that's what I gave them. I met up with them, took them out and invested in them. I also gathered a few of the key young people in the church and asked them to show kindness and give Billy and Louise a chance. In time, Billy and Louise relaxed, and the youth group became a safe place for them—a place where they could spiritually grow. Ultimately it became their family.

This is what the church is supposed to be!

Our churches should welcome people of faith and no faith. In order to get to know God, people often need to get to know us first. They need to feel comfortable, wanted and accepted for who they are. And Christians are uniquely placed to offer a non-judgmental, warm, friendly community. Why? Because we also offer something much greater than that. We can provide the opportunity to become not just part of the community but part of the family—God's family. A family of people made in the image of God, welcomed as one, in the pursuit of the Creator.

When Paul wrote to the Ephesians, he pointed out that they were known as "uncircumcised", whereas the Jews were "the circumcision", meaning they were part of God's historic people who held a covenant with God (Ephesians 2:11-12). Gentiles and Jews seemed like entirely separate groups. However, Paul wrote that in Christ these distinctions didn't matter anymore.

Jesus "has made the two groups one and has destroyed the barrier, the dividing wall of hostility" (v 14). Jew and Gentile could unite as one in Christ. So could rich and poor, educated and uneducated, haves and have-nots, "spiritual" and "unspiritual".

> *So now you [Billy and Louise] are no longer strangers and foreigners. You are citizens along with all of God's holy people. You are members of God's family.*
>
> *(Ephesians 2:19, NLT)*

Because of Christ, Billy and Louise could be equals in a wealthy church. Their status did not depend on their affluence or lack of it. Instead it was marked out by the blood of Jesus and the unity of the Holy Spirit. They were no longer strangers and foreigners, but members of God's family. Through Jesus and an acceptance of him, they became children of God (John 1:12).

### Becoming God's Children

Chelsea had been in the same foster family—alongside her two birth sisters—for as long as Steph had known her, starting from the age of eleven.

Throughout her high-school years, Chelsea was a regular at the lunchtime club and after-school youth café that Steph and her team ran. Her presence was consistent, and as the years went on, the hard shell she had built up to protect herself began to soften as staff and volunteers valued her and encouraged her creativity. She even came along to the summer camps.

Then everything changed. When Chelsea was 16, her foster family suddenly moved away, leaving her behind.

By 17, they had completely cut ties with her. That was the moment the stability she'd known for much of her childhood crumbled. Chelsea began to bounce between temporary foster placements and sheltered living arrangements, none of them permanent and each one a little more uncertain.

But Chelsea was a Christian—she had been about 15 when Steph had had the privilege of leading her to Christ via email during the Covid pandemic. Their connection deepened from that point on. With permission, Steph continued to mentor Chelsea online, walking with her through each new placement and change of address. Wherever Chelsea ended up, Steph worked to help her find a local church. And in one of those churches, Steph was honoured to be invited to baptise her—a sacred moment that stood out in an otherwise unsettled journey.

On Chelsea's 18th birthday, Steph made the hour-and-a-half journey to a deprived community where Chelsea had been placed in sheltered living accommodation. She was alone—with no friends, no family and no celebration. Steph arrived with a present and a cake, doing what she could to make Chelsea feel seen.

When I met Chelsea, she was a leader at the camp I was speaking at. She was now 19, employed and pushing deeper into her faith. I would never have guessed what Chelsea had been through. She was well-adjusted, mature and engaging.

Chelsea's is a story of what a transformed life can look like. She met Jesus and became part of God's family. The impact on her was profound! But don't miss one of the most important factors in her story: Steph. Chelsea needed more than an understanding of the gospel and commitment to Jesus. She needed God's people.

Steph developed an authentic relationship with Chelsea—she cared and was interested in her life. If Chelsea had never become a Christian, it wouldn't have changed her relationship with Steph. In other words, she was not a project for conversion. Steph was being a witness (Acts 1:8) and a disciple who makes disciples (Matthew 28:19). She lived out the sentiment Paul expressed to the Thessalonians: "Because we loved you so much, we were delighted to share with you not only the gospel of God but our lives as well" (1 Thessalonians 2:8).

Chelsea's discovery of belonging started with Steph. Then it moved to a church community, where she was able to experience more fully what it means to be part of God's family.

Look at the following verse through the eyes of someone like Chelsea:

> *God decided in advance to adopt us into his own family by bringing us to himself through Jesus Christ. This is what he wanted to do, and it gave him great pleasure.*
> *(Ephesians 1:5, NLT)*

God wanted to adopt Chelsea, who had only ever known what it meant to be fostered. Can you imagine how powerful and significant that must have been for her? It is just as significant whether a young person is from the care system, a single-parent home or a blended family—or indeed a home with both biological parents. Being adopted into God's family is a profound and transformative privilege. And we have an opportunity to share this privilege with a new generation.

**Welcome the Wild**

However, I would be wrong to give the impression that this is always going to be easy.

Anyone who has ever belonged to a family knows that there is always an assortment of personalities. Some sweet, some tangy, some mild, some bitter and some that can only be described as "unusual" or "an acquired taste". When we welcome those who are new to church, that's how our congregations are going to look too.

Unchurched young people have no understanding of church culture; they don't know the rules. They are not used to sitting still and following the set processes that are so familiar to us in our church services and youth work—whether it's modern songs, prayers and a sermon, a liturgical service that follows the Book of Common Prayer, or a Friday youth night with a talk and discussion groups. This is unfamiliar ground, and young people are likely to do the "wrong" thing, whether deliberately or accidentally. They may expect to be allowed to actively participate—and do so in a way that causes disruption. They may find it hard to sit still. Not every unchurched young person is disruptive, of course—but don't assume that they are necessarily going to be easy to have in your church!

But come with me to Luke 5. Jesus is teaching. He has an attentive audience. He is in full flow—and then something dramatic happens. A bunch of men want to bring a paralysed man to Jesus, but...

> *When they could not find a way to do this because of the crowd, they went up on the roof and lowered him on his mat through the tiles into the middle of the crowd, right in front of Jesus. (Luke 5:19)*

There are two things to note. First, these men have damaged someone's property. They lowered their friend "through the tiles"—in other words, they have made a hole in the roof! Second, they have disrupted Jesus in the middle of his teaching.

This account got me thinking.

Have I brought unchurched young people to church who have ended up causing damage to the property? Box ticked, yes.

Have I watched young people do something that resulted in the preacher having to stop his message to address the disruption? That's a tick, yes.

Have I been told by the pastor not to bring those young people back again? Sadly, it's another tick, yes.

But is that how Jesus responded?

> *When Jesus saw their faith, he said, "Friend, your sins are forgiven." (v 20)*

Jesus could have been annoyed by the disruption to his message and the damage to the building, but he wasn't. Instead, he focused on the need right in front of him. And who is to say that a disruptive young person isn't seeking Jesus?

### It's Worth It

Are we willing to embrace disruption and dysfunction? If people are to join the church family from a diversity of backgrounds, is the church willing to make a few adjustments to help them feel part of the family?

If you are the pastor or the elder of your church, then I wonder if you would take a moment to ask and answer this question: what is most important to me—a neat and orderly service where everyone is happy, or giving unchurched young people an opportunity to absorb something of Jesus and explore joining the family? Same question if you are the youth pastor or a youth leader. Unchurched young people may bring a level of chaos to a well-oiled programme. Are you willing to allow that to happen?

If you are not a pastor or elder, or not the main youth leader, then I want to encourage you to have that very conversation with your church leaders. You need their backing if you wish to reach out to young people in the community.

Let me circle back to my first story: the one of the two young people whose mum was now dating someone close to their own age. Can you imagine the pain they might bring with them, and how that might play out in a church setting? What of Billy and Louise, who started fights because they felt that they didn't fit the middle-class nature of the church? How about Chelsea before she gave her life to Jesus, having lived the life that she had, where even her foster family disconnected from her—can you imagine some of the relational challenges she may have brought?

We all love the end of the story of the paralysed man:

> *[Jesus] said to the paralysed man, "I tell you, get up, take your mat and go home." Immediately he stood up*

*in front of them, took what he had been lying on and went home praising God. (Luke 5:24-25)*

Amazing! But what about the broken roof and disrupted sermon?

Before people can belong, they need to be welcomed and accepted with warts and all. Once they are accepted, they will start to feel secure. Once they are secure, they will start to trust, and when that happens, they will want to stay. It happens by God's grace, but it also happens because of what we do to welcome them.

How much do we want unchurched young people to reach a place where they feel they belong and want to stay? It may cost us something, but a transformed life is worth it every time. When that happens, you will see the same response that the crowd has in Luke 5:

*Everyone was amazed and gave praise to God. They were filled with awe and said, "We have seen remarkable things today." (Luke 5:26)*

### A Note on Safeguarding

I have talked a lot about the importance of developing relationships with young people, but this needs to happen within appropriate boundaries. Make sure you have the following things in place:

- Every volunteer should have a DBS (England & Wales), PVG (Scotland), or Access NI (Northern Ireland) check. This ensures that nobody has previously been barred from working with young people. It's also a good idea to take up references.

- Conduct safeguarding training to ensure that all your volunteers know how to protect young people and spot warning signs.
- Devise appropriate safeguarding guidelines for your setting. If you don't have a policy already, consider contacting the Christian safeguarding charity Thirtyone:eight for help.

Chapter 5

# Gen Z-A and Morality

**I SAT RECENTLY** with a distraught Christian mum. She had raised her children to believe that marriage was for one man and one woman, but her son, now in his later teens, had shared that he was gay. He dismissed God and was sad that his mum couldn't "love all of him, but only some of him". For that teenager, theology was deeply personal, and since he perceived that it rejected him, he felt he had no choice but to reject God. His mum told me that she felt guilty for the damage she had caused to her son.

What was happening here? It comes from a shift in our culture's understanding of morality. Do you believe that there is an objective standard based on absolute truth which determines good and bad, right or wrong, in a way that is not dependent on anyone's interpretation? Or do you believe that "truths" around good and bad are more subjective than that—what's good for me is different from what's good for you, and each of us gets to decide for ourselves? Increasingly,

Western people believe the latter, particularly Gen Z-A. They are firm believers that they are the authors of their values and choices, and they don't take kindly to other forms of authority imposing values and decisions upon them.

That mum had stuck to what she believed to be the objective truth about sexuality. But her son saw this as a rejection of who he was as a person. The way he saw it, she was imposing values and lifestyle decisions on him, and that's deeply wrong.

This change in people's understanding of morality is happening within the church as well as outside it. Subjective morality is seeping deep and creating a level of turbulence between Gen Z and older generations. Intriguingly, older Gen Z and younger Millennial churchgoers are more likely to read their Bible than other generations, but they are also more likely to have problems with what they are reading, as well as to be shaken by cultural opposition to the Bible.[23] Gone are the days when what a pastor teaches is generally accepted without question. Younger generations are scrutinising anything deemed intolerant. *Why are you preaching that God is so judgmental? Why do you, in your sermon, get to tell me how I should live and what I should believe?* For many of them, it just doesn't compute that a good God would insist on values and ways of life that seem completely outdated.

You and I know that if anyone has the right to tell us how to live, then it is the Creator God, who *is* good and *does* have our best interests at heart. In a world of "your truth" and "my truth", Jesus is *the* truth. Somehow, that's both beautifully simple to comprehend and at times exceptionally complex to navigate!

So how do we communicate it?

### A Progressive Generation

It might surprise you to hear that many social commentators are having their attention caught by the growing *conservative* nature of Gen Z. They are less likely to sleep around, view (classic) porn or binge-drink; they are increasingly likely to warm to traditional values and be more risk-averse. But according to the *New Statesman*, "There is one clear outlier when it comes to Gen Z's conservative tendencies, and that is their fluidity around sexuality and gender."[24]

The UK national census in 2021 revealed that 6.9% of 16-24-year-olds identify as LGB+, compared with 0.4% of over-75-year-olds.[25] When it comes to gender, "16 to 24 year olds are twice as likely to identify as trans as the general population."[26] In America, Pew Research found that almost 60% of Gen Z felt that "other" should be an option on forms that ask about people's gender.[27] The More in Common think tank discovered that 62% of Gen Z in the UK believed the statement that a trans man is a man and a trans woman is a woman.[28]

Young people may be latching on to conservative values, but they are very progressive on matters of identity and sexuality. So where does this leave us?

The orthodox biblical view of gender is that God created humanity as male and female (Genesis 1:27)—there are two genders, and these are God-given. Regarding sexuality, the Bible teaches that sex is a gift from God, intended only for within marriage between one man and one woman (Genesis 2:24; Matthew 19:4-6). In all things, believers are called to honour God with their bodies, desires and identity (1 Corinthians 6:19-20).

God's design for our bodies and our sexuality is good! We can trust him that this is the path to flourishing and that obedience to his ways is always right. But given what we know about Gen Z-A's progressive views, we can probably agree that the biblical view of sexuality and gender is not the *first* thing an unbelieving young person needs to hear about Christianity.

As a child, I couldn't swallow various foods; they just wouldn't go down. So my mum avoided giving them to me until I was older. It wasn't that she gave me a complete pass on these foods—rather, she circled back to them when I was able to swallow them without instinctively gagging or choking. My mum didn't give me an ultimatum—"Eat this or you will never eat!" Rather, she was patient, kind, compassionate and understanding. Her priority was for me to eat.

What is our priority for young people? It should be for them to experience the joy of God's presence. We do want to teach them the whole truth about God and not give them a pass on the bits they don't like. So at the right point, there will be a need to circle back to topics like sexuality and gender—we would be wrong not to communicate what the Bible says about these things. We would also be wrong to actively try to hide what the Bible says and be dishonest about it because we're afraid of the possible reaction. But there is no need to push people to swallow something they can't. Let's help them enjoy God in whatever way they best connect with, first. Then circle back later.

A few years ago, some colleagues and I were running an induction week for young adults who had signed up to spend a year volunteering with Youth for Christ. We were staying at a residential centre where other groups were also staying. One of those groups was made up of young people who were gender transitioning.

Every evening, we would gather our Year Out students for a worship time. One night, as I was heading out of the hall for a comfort break, I spotted a young person from the gender-transitioning group sitting on the floor in the corridor, eyes closed, engaged in the worship coming from the hall I had just left.

What I witnessed in that brief moment seemed no different to how many of our Year Outs were also engaging on the other side of the wall. There was no doubt in my mind that the young person in the corridor was genuinely connecting with God.

My point in telling this story is simply this: we must avoid the temptation to disregard those who don't fit neatly within our theological framework. I am often reminded of the saying attributed to Billy Graham: "It is the Holy Spirit's job to convict, God's job to judge and my job to love". If God can engage with a young person in the corridor like that, he can also move their heart and address the barriers that they have put up.

The reality is that an unchurched young person with progressive views on sexuality is no more or less a sinner than the best-behaved churchgoing teenager. We *all* need the saving work of Jesus, and any of us can receive it. The wave of the Holy Spirit will move far and wide!

### What God Cares About

Of course, you will have conversations about gender and sexuality at some point—and we'll come back to that in a moment. But first I want to show you that the bigger picture of what Gen Z-A care about actually has a surprising amount in common with what the Bible says God cares about.

Gen Z-A's values are rooted in empathy. They prize tolerance above all in the belief that self-expression is sacred. They look at the past and see examples of where one person imposing their viewpoint on another led to oppression and a lack of opportunities. They care.

They believe in justice, by which they often mean standing up for those who can't stand up for themselves. They are concerned about mercy and showing kindness and compassion. They also put a value on the experiential—what "your truth" is depends on what you have experienced in your life.

What does God think about these values?

> *He has shown you, O mortal, what is good. And what does the LORD require of you? To act justly and to love mercy and to walk humbly with your God.*
>
> *(Micah 6:8)*

This verse begins, "He has shown you, O mortal, what is good." There *is* an objective morality. What God says is good *is* good, regardless of what I think and feel about it. He calls us to trust him about that. To trust what the Bible says and try to live the way God says is right.

Take a look, though, at what God calls good: justice, mercy, humility, and walking closely with him, not just in belief but in daily lived experience. That sounds a lot like the heartbeat of Gen Z-A. Sure, it's not a perfect overlap, but it's a meaningful starting point.

So don't lose heart just because Gen Z-A values self-expression or leans toward subjective truth. Yes, they may hold views that feel unfamiliar or uncomfortable. However, by and large they also long for a world marked by compassion, fairness and humility. These values are a reflection (if an imperfect one) of God's values. And so they open the door for us to show Gen Z-A that God's way isn't just true—it's good.

### Introducing a Good God

Imagine you're talking to a young person about God. They don't know much about him, but they're interested to find out. Gently, you might try asking these very simple exploratory questions:

- "What do you think God cares about?" (If they don't know, then rephrase it: "If you created the world, what would you care about?")
- "Why do you think/feel that?" (This is really the power question—it's where you get to learn and discover where they're coming from.)
- "Would you say that your values and God's values are the same? Why?" (You may not need to ask this one depending on what they have said.)

- "Do you want to see what God says about what he cares about?"

Then you might draw their attention to some of the following verses.

| WHAT Z-A CARE ABOUT | WHAT GOD SAYS ABOUT IT | REFERENCES |
|---|---|---|
| Homelessness | Share your food; provide shelter for the needy; take care of the homeless. | • Isaiah 58:7<br>• Leviticus 25:35-36<br>• Matthew 25:35 |
| Poverty | Those who are kind to the needy are honouring God. | • Proverbs 14:31<br>• Luke 11:41<br>• Deuteronomy 15:11 |
| Racism | Partiality (discrimination/ racism) is wrong. | • James 2:1-4<br>• Galatians 3:28<br>• Luke 10:25-37 |
| Immigration | Treat foreigners as if they were born in the nation they now live; love them as yourself. | • Leviticus 19:34<br>• Hebrews 13:1-2<br>• Ephesians 2:19 |
| War and Terror | Love your enemy; live at peace with everyone; turn the other cheek. | • Matthew 5:44<br>• Romans 12:18<br>• Matthew 5:39 |

| | | |
|---|---|---|
| Climate and Environment | God made the earth and was pleased; everything on and in the earth belongs to God; we should take care of it. | • Genesis 1:31<br>• Psalm 24:1<br>• Genesis 2:15 |
| Sexuality | Sexuality is a sacred and beautiful gift, designed for bonding a man and a woman in lifelong union. | • Genesis 2:20-24<br>• Hebrews 13:4<br>• 1 Timothy 1:9-11 |
| Loneliness | God is a father to the fatherless and a defender of widows, and places the lonely in families. | • Psalm 68:5<br>• Psalm 23:4<br>• Matthew 28:20 |
| Justice | Demonstrate justice, mercy and compassion. | • Zechariah 7:9<br>• Proverbs 29:7<br>• Matthew 12:18 |

Today's young people often have an acute awareness of brokenness in society. Take Black Lives Matter, Me Too, the pulling down of statues, the response to the conflict in Gaza, the need to defend the immigrants and refugees targeted in the Southport riots... It all speaks to something being broken and Z-A's desire to oppose toxicity. Showing Gen Z-A that God cares about the brokenness in society is going to go a long way to convince them that he really is good—and that he *should* have the final word about how we live.

Once you've discussed some of the topics above, it might then become possible to talk on a more personal level about morality and introduce the idea of sin. Perhaps the conversation will go like this (but in language that makes sense to the individual):

- If society has aspects of brokenness, then logically we must also, to some degree, have our own elements of personal brokenness. Human goodness is fragile. It has to be, because society has proved to be and continues to be broken, and society is made up of individuals.
- Personal and societal brokenness create a wedge between the holy and perfect God and his creation, including us.
- Ultimately, Jesus was broken on a cross for our brokenness, which we call sin.
- Jesus died on the cross because he cares about us. We are broken, but he wants to bring us healing and wholeness.

Can you see how this is a way to communicate about sin in terms that Gen Z-A will understand? The good news of the gospel is that Christ died to take the punishment for our sin, but that may not appear good news if you believe people are inherently good and that we should all choose our own morality. Young people may not instinctively see that they are in need of a Saviour for their "wrongness". By contrast, the starting point of "brokenness" can make much more sense as a way in to understanding the nature of sin and therefore see the wonderful goodness of Jesus in salvation. This might not be all you would ever want to say to someone about the nature of sin, but it's a starting point that will connect.

**Gracious Listening**

Leading a devotion for a crowd of youth leaders, I asked the question: "Is it right to watch a sex scene within a TV show? Didn't Jesus say that if you even look at another lustfully, then you are committing adultery?"

I followed up with the invitation to disagree with me. I could be wrong, but I wanted them to try and present an alternative perspective by using the Bible.

I had a line of younger leaders (all Gen Z and younger Millennials) knocking at my door, and each conversation started like this: "I can't argue from a biblical perspective, but you're not right! I can watch a sex scene and not be remotely impacted by it." It was a textbook example of how Gen Z tends to see morality. A high value is placed on tolerance (you shouldn't impose a viewpoint on me) and on personal experience (that doesn't happen to me, so it isn't true).

The invitation led to some honest, meaningful conversations. More than anything else, I was curious, I was ready to learn and I listened. I pointed us back to the Bible at various moments and created space for truth to be explored and worked through together.

Any person will feel valued and loved when we can show that we are primarily interested in them rather than in being the expert and winning the discussion. When we listen and share in this open way, something wonderful occurs: we start to connect with their head *and* heart! Gracious listening allows for truth to be shared and the Spirit to move.

### Leading a Discussion

Gender and sexuality are weighty topics. You'll need to go to other books if you want a fuller understanding of what the Bible says about this area and how it relates to the view of today's secular culture.[29] I don't have space to do these issues justice here. I would just encourage you not to be afraid of talking about them when the moment is right!

The key, once again, is to carefully *listen*, and then consider how Jesus' good news can best be communicated to the young people you've listened to. I want to encourage you to foster an environment where young people are safe to ask their big questions—about sexuality and anything else.

In many cases, young people may want to discuss as a group rather than individually. A discussion group needs some basic guidelines to ensure it remains a safe and helpful environment.

- Set a length of time, and give a 5- or 10-minute warning when you are almost finished so that it doesn't feel that you cut the meeting off abruptly. This way, people won't feel shut down or overlooked.

- Go out of your way to emphasise that it's a conversation, not a debate. It isn't about scoring points. So tone is key. There will be no raised voices, no matter how passionate people might feel, and everyone has the right to seek clarity on what was just said.

- Establish rules around phones. If you allow them, people might wish to record the conversation—if so, make sure there is an agreement that the recording won't be edited or played on social media out of context. If you decide to have no phones so that people feel safe and free to talk, encourage them to invite an adult they trust so that it doesn't appear you are suppressing or controlling the conversation.

- Yes or no questions are discouraged. Instead encourage questions that allow for context and for the person to feel fully heard.

- Ask more questions than you answer. Not as an avoidance tactic, but so that you understand the concerns and emotions being felt. Be sensitive to the reality that any question or view may be a lived experience for someone in the room.

- Be encouraging, supportive, affirming and respectful. When people are upset or feel you have said something you didn't say, don't push back hard—recognise that pain is being felt and that the kindest thing you can do is take a posture of humility.

- When wrapping up, ask how everyone is doing and whether anything has caused upset or insult. Listen carefully. If unintended upset has occurred, encourage very clear apologies and discourage a defensive "No, I never actually said that..." response. End well and leave as friends with an invitation to meet again.

Give it a few weeks, and don't be surprised if you're having conversations that you might expect to be having in a house group or youth discipleship group around prayer or belief or miracles. Remember, this is a spiritually open generation!

### The Friend of Sinners, the Source of Wisdom

One final reflection on the mum I mentioned at the start of the chapter. Her deep sense of regret didn't come from changing her mind on sexuality but on looking back at the version of Jesus she had presented to her son. She realised that the faith she had modelled was harsh and judgmental. She didn't wish that she'd taught her son something different about morality, but she did wish she'd taught him a truer picture of the Jesus we see on the pages of the Gospels—the Jesus who is full of kindness, love, compassion and understanding.

That doesn't make it any less of a complex challenge for us to navigate those issues where beliefs and values are seemingly in conflict. It can seem intimidating to address such big topics because we don't want to be misunderstood. We also don't want to compromise on biblical truth, which we know is ultimately always good news. Perhaps the best way to get through this minefield is to focus on Jesus—inviting young people to encounter him as he really is: the friend of sinners.

Still unsure? Here's what the Bible says we should do about such issues:

> *If any of you lacks wisdom, you should ask God, who gives generously to all without finding fault, and it will be given to you. (James 1:5)*

Let's listen to young people, but most of all let's listen to God.

Chapter 6

# Gen Z-A and Value

**IN A TRANSACTIONAL** world, everything has value, including people.

The value a club places on a football player's transfer fee; the amount we are willing to pay for a ticket to see an artist perform at a concert; the quantity of time we give to watching the reels of online influencers. They all speak of value.

I once found myself backstage at an event in New York. I was about to share the stage with a few other folk in an interview about youth work. Then Tim Keller, the well-known author, pastor and speaker, would follow on straight after our interview. As I waited to be called up, I saw Keller just a few feet away, and I watched person after person seek him out, introduce themselves and pass on their details. What struck me was the time, interest and engagement he gave back to them. I asked someone who knew him whether he grew tired of that—the reply was "He will always make himself accessible!"

Tim Keller was a very big deal! He sold millions of books and spoke at all the big events. His value on the Christian scene was very high. However, to him, so was the importance of every person who came to shake his hand and take up his time before he had to go on stage to speak to a crowd of thousands of people.

Another time, I organised an international conference, and I was responsible for inviting speakers. A very renowned speaker sent on his terms, which included first-class travel and a five-star hotel. His note explained that we had a choice: each day, he would either preach for 30 minutes, or he would mingle and say hello to people for 30 minutes. It was one or the other. This speaker had placed a very high value on himself.

Contrast that with Keller. Even better, contrast it with Jesus, who humbled himself to become a human, be born in a stable, ride a donkey, and serve rather than be served, which ultimately resulted in his execution. The value Jesus so powerfully demonstrated was not placed on himself but on humanity!

### Who Am I, and Do I Matter?

For most young people, the way others see them helps to form a sense of their own value and their own identity. What are they good at? For what reasons do others show interest in them? At an early age, we begin to confuse our identity with what we do or how we look, and this carries on throughout life. Labels form who we are. An A* pupil, a dropout, a bully, an athlete. Labels create a sense of value or a lack of value. They stick, and even when we pull them off, the residue remains.

Identity and value are deeply intertwined. The natural development of a young person is to try and establish both their identity and sense of worth. Ever wondered what drives a top student to study night after night, or a teenage swimmer to get up at 5 a.m. every morning to hit the pool before school in the hope of winning the county trophy? It's not only to gain some kind of satisfaction but also to establish their identity and value.

I once had an 18-year-old girl in my youth group whose presence stirred a lot of attention—and concern. Her outfits often pushed boundaries, and her behaviour towards the boys in the group was noticeably flirtatious, sometimes crossing lines that made others uncomfortable. She spoke openly and confidently about her aim never to marry, explaining that she saw no point in committing to one person. It became clear that she was involved in multiple relationships at a physical level and didn't hide it—in fact, she often spoke about it with boldness and even pride.

At first glance, it was easy to label this girl's behaviour as provocative or rebellious. But as I got to know her, I realised she was carrying something much deeper. In a conversation, I asked her what drove her need to be so relationally active. Her answer has never left me:

> *It's the one thing I know I'm good at. It's where I get my value. When I'm wanted, I feel like I matter.*

Behind the bravado was a longing to be seen, valued and chosen. And while she may have gained both her identity and a sense of value from her sexual activity, the pain in her eyes was evident. What looked like confidence was actually a cry for worth.

Here's an admirable quality of Z-A: they are driven by a belief that people matter. They care about ending racism and homelessness and addressing immigration—and the reason why they care is because they believe people are valuable. The same principle lies behind their wish to respect a person's choices about sexuality and gender. They believe that to disagree with someone's chosen gender is to say they are not valuable as a person.

You can see how important it is that we communicate to young people that they matter—that they are deeply valued.

## We Matter to Jesus

It's not hard to see that Jesus valued the people he encountered. Take for example this account:

> *A woman was there who had been subject to bleeding for twelve years, but no one could heal her.*
>
> *(Luke 8:43)*

We are drawn to the lady's medical condition—what did it mean that she bled? And how sad it was that she had suffered for so long without a cure! But we may miss an important factor: she would likely have been crippled by her identity and her sense of worthlessness. In Judaism, under the law, when a woman had her menstrual cycle, she was seen as "unclean" for that period of time and had to avoid the places and people she would normally go to in order not to contaminate others. This woman had been bleeding for twelve years; she must have been ostracised, living on the margins. She was perpetually unclean.

> *She came up behind him and touched the edge of his cloak, and immediately her bleeding stopped.*
>
> *"Who touched me?" Jesus asked.*
>
> *When they all denied it, Peter said, "Master, the people are crowding and pressing against you." (v 44-45)*

That's awesome—she was instantly healed! However, don't miss the hugely significant reality of what happened. There was a crowd. That means this woman had come out from the edges of society to the centre—she was in public. She defied the law even further by pushing through the crowd to get to Jesus. That meant she touched people. Under the law she was considered unclean. Her identity was uncleanness, and by touching others she was making them unclean too.

> *But Jesus said, "Someone touched me; I know that power has gone out from me." (v 46)*

There was even more to this scene than a wonderful healing, and Jesus knew it. When an unclean woman touched Jesus, according to the law she made him unclean. However, that doesn't seem to be what actually happened. Instead, it was the woman who was made clean by touching Jesus.

> *Then the woman, seeing that she could not go unnoticed, came trembling and fell at his feet. In the presence of all the people, she told why she had touched him and how she had been instantly healed. Then*

> *[Jesus] said to her, "Daughter, your faith has healed you. Go in peace." (v 47-48)*

Why was she trembling? Surely because her identity as an unclean woman who had breached the law was about to be exposed! The whole crowd would have been perplexed by her explanation. Was this good (since she'd been healed) or bad (since she'd broken their customs and law)?

But Jesus gave the woman dignity and saw her true value as a beautiful human being made in the image of God, now free of her stigma. It wasn't her illness that defined her but being made in the image of God, and it was her belief in Jesus that set her free.

Whether a young person gains their self-worth and identity from what they do or don't do, who they are or who they are not, how they look or don't look, what they have done or haven't done, Jesus sees past all of that. Just as with the bleeding woman, he sees their true value as a beautiful human being—marred, yes, but fundamentally made in the image of God.

**Life to the Full**

There are millions of young people questioning their identity and worth—millions crippled by self-doubt and uncertain of whether they matter to anybody.

Remember John 10:10: the thief comes to steal, kill and destroy!

The lies spoken over young people can be overwhelming. The schoolteacher who states they are not clever enough or won't amount to much in life. The harassment received in response to a selfie posted online, with people commenting "ugly" or "fat" or "whore". The teenager with neurodiversity challenges who is branded as a weirdo for staring a fraction longer than others might or giving a factual response to an emotional issue. The shy or introverted young person who is excluded from parties because it's assumed they don't like people. The teen who is taunted as useless and left out of football games or relegated to positions no one else wants to play. Those on free school lunches who are seen as the poor kids with lazy parents who live off benefits rather than wanting to work. On the list goes, all speaking to value and all forming someone's identity, forming an opinion confirmed by the whispers of the enemy: "You don't matter."

If it seems a little dramatic to suggest such lies go so far as to steal, kill and destroy, perhaps a simple statistic might convince you otherwise: according to Samaritans, roughly 200 young people end their lives in the UK each year.[30] That means that in the next 36 hours or so, a young person is likely to end their life. These are not insignificant numbers! I would suggest that it isn't dramatic to state that the enemy's whispers are killing, stealing and destroying young people's lives. In fact, I propose that that is exactly what is happening.

There is a war occurring on the streets, in the schools and in the homes of young people all across our nation. It is a battle between light and darkness, good and evil, right and wrong!

But Jesus said, "I have come that they may have life, and have it to the full." Jesus has come to speak life over us and to remind us of just how valuable we are! Jesus has a message for every young person: *You matter, you are important, and you are wanted!*

That is a wonderful starting point of good news for Z-A.

### Communicating Value

As a starting point, there are three very simple ways that we can help a young person feel valued:

- Learn and remember their name. When you see them, call them directly by their name. There is power in this very simple gesture.
- Learn something about them—something that matters to them. I once had a teenager obsessed with the Barbie movie, so I watched it too. It definitely wasn't my kind of movie, but I happily chatted with the young person about all the key points. The reason why I knew it had made a difference was that I had eye contact and a smile from that young person for the first time.
- Be present, not distracted. Most likely, every person a teenager knows has a device in their hand and is head down, busy scrolling or messaging. Break the trend! See them, affirm them, pay attention to them and give them as long as they need.

These three things might seem obvious, but you will be amazed by how easy it is to miss two or even all three of them. My first ever youth group that I attended as a teenager had eight young people and was led by a priest. When I joined, he asked what my name was, and I happily informed him. The following week, the priest vaguely recognised me and asked again for my name. I again informed him. The week after, the same thing: “What’s your name?” This went on for eight weeks!

I then joined a different youth group—this one had 30-40 people attending. The youth leader already knew who I was before I walked through the door, and greeted me by name, enquiring about my week and what was coming up. The following week, I was asked how the various things I had mentioned had worked out. The leader noticed when I had a haircut or new clothes.

The experience of my first youth group left me feeling as if I didn’t matter. When there were only eight people, yet after eight weeks the leader couldn’t remember my name, it left the distinct impression of a lack of interest in me! The other group, however, was completely different. There I felt valued, included and wanted.

I have long since come to understand that at a surface level, our names equal our identity and worth. If you cannot learn someone’s name, then that individual will not feel that they matter to you. Almost certainly, the priest who couldn’t remember my name had memory challenges, and I understand that. But he could have written my name down and taken out the piece of paper to remind himself the following week—then I would have known I mattered enough for him to *want* to know my name even though it was tricky to remember it. I guarantee that if you do this, it will speak volumes.

### The Long Game

Let me go back to that 18-year-old who engaged in physical relationships and hit on a number of boys in the youth group. Together with other leaders, I worked hard to journey with her and to show her how valuable she was and how much she mattered. It didn't seem to make any impact at all. Eventually, my job changed, and I ended up moving country. But a number of years later, I received an email from this girl completely out of the blue. It went something like this:

> *I just wanted you to know that I am now happily married, and I am faithful. You were a big part in helping me change. You made me feel like I had value, and helped me find Jesus.*

I cannot even begin to describe how that email made me feel!

Simply demonstrating that people matter may not seem like very much, but it can make an enormous difference. I can't change young people's circumstances, and I might never see how their lives turn out, but this is not going to stop me from calling them by their name, learning about what matters to them, and being fully present whenever I am with them. The rest is over to the Holy Spirit.

Just by reading this far into the book, you have shown that you care about young people. Go a step further, if you haven't already, by demonstrating in these very simple ways that they really do matter to you.

# 3
# Looking Wide

Chapter 7

# Gen Z-A and Digital Technology

"**WHY ARE YOUNG** people always on devices?"

It's not an uncommon question, perhaps most often asked by Boomers to Gen X and Millennial parents.

The answer is a very simple one: we, the adults, put the devices into their hands, and we have encouraged them to fill their time looking at screens! We just hadn't necessarily thought through where it may lead.

In 2012, it was estimated that anyone born that year would spend one full year watching screen media by the time they were seven.[31] In other words, of the 61,320 hours they would have lived by their seventh birthday, 8,760 of those would have been spent on a screen watching some form of media! Those born from 2010 onwards are considered Gen Alpha, and are truly digital natives. We have taught this generation that digital technology is an integral, crucial part of their lives. If you need more proof, consider that in the US in

2024, 49% of Gen Alpha—that's nearly half of everyone between the ages of 0 and 14—owned a tablet.[32] In America, the average 11-14-year-old spends around 9 hours in front of a screen every day.[33] That includes 3 hours 16 minutes watching TV or videos, 1 hour 46 minutes gaming, 1 hour 27 minutes on social media, 51 minutes browsing the internet, 20 minutes video chatting, 15 minutes e-reading and 14 minutes creating content for others to view.[34]

All of this raises the question: where are young people's key influences coming from in their most formative years? Not from school. Some of their screen time will take place within an educational institution but only a small proportion.

If we are to continue in our journey of understanding, welcoming and caring for Z-A, we need to consider the role of digital technology and social media in their lives. Here's a spoiler alert: both have a profound impact on young people's mental wellbeing.

In the next three chapters, I want to outline a few aspects of these three facets of Gen Z-A's world—digital tech, social media and mental health. We'll focus on the challenges young people are facing in these areas and consider what we can do to help them. First, technology.

### Behaviour and Addiction

If I told you that the blue light emitted by your smartphone, tablet or computer screen could help with depression in winter, improve acne and other skin conditions and even boost memory, you might be suspicious of my sources. Well, don't take my word for it—check it out for yourself![35]

If that is really the case, shouldn't we be advocating for more time in front of our screens than less time? Blue light seems like a good thing. Except for the fact that it messes with sleep. It causes us to take longer to fall asleep, suppresses melatonin, impacts REM (rapid eye movement), which is essential for deep sleep and cognitive abilities, and reduces alertness in the morning.[36] Hmm.

Recent studies have found that 75% of children and 70% of adults use electronic devices in their bedroom or bed.[37] If we do stream in bed, then we can expect a disrupted night. The odd disrupted night is okay, of course—just expect to be grumpy in the morning! But lots of disrupted nights will start to play havoc with our cognitive abilities, memory and emotional wellbeing.

You have probably heard the word "dopamine" bandied about in connection with technology. Dopamine is a neurotransmitter in the brain that is nicknamed "the feel-good molecule"; it provides a pleasurable reward sensation. Every time we receive a notification or achieve an objective within a game, we receive a dopamine hit in our brains, making us immediately feel good, just for a brief moment.

The problem is that our brains were not created to receive so many hits. Through continual scrolling, checking messages and gaming, we become addicted—the same thing is happening in our brains as what happens when we get addicted to alcohol or drugs. The result is that we reach for our pleasure devices over and over again, to the point where we do it without even realising it. We pick up our phone, open an app, close it, open a different app, close it, and then return to the first app we closed less than three seconds ago. Why do we do that?

Anna Lembke, a professor of psychiatry and behavioural sciences at Stanford University, explains it like this:

> *With repeated use, our brains adapt by downgrading dopamine transmission ... With enough ongoing exposure, our brains enter a dopamine deficit state, characterised by depression, anxiety, insomnia, irritability and craving. Once that happens, we're reaching for digital media, not as a tool to accomplish a specific task ... but to get out of the dopamine deficit state and stop feeling bad.*[38]

According to Common Sense Media, 50% of young people believe they are addicted to their mobile devices, and 59% of their parents believe their teens are addicted.[39] Society has a very real problem when half of an entire demographic admits it has an addiction! Young people often have an unhealthy dependence on technology. The question for us is: how do we address this with them?

You might wonder, "Why does it matter?" If our purpose is simply to share the good news of Jesus, why do we need to bother about smartphones? For two reasons. One is that screen addiction is going to affect the way we interact with Gen Z-A. We need to think practically about how to manage or regulate their use of phones while we are with them, and we need to understand how digital technology can impact the way they interact with us even when they don't actually have their phones out. The other reason stems from what we have discussed in the previous few chapters. We need to show Gen Z-A that we *care*. The thief comes to steal, kill and destroy, but Jesus came so that people might have life to the full! If we want to show Gen Z-A that life to the full really is on offer, we need to be talking to them about how their screens are impacting their lives.

### Attention and Concentration

There is growing evidence to suggest that the very brains of children and young people are being altered due to digital technologies. In an article for *The Independent*, Dr Samir Shah, a consultant psychiatrist and medical director at the Priory Hospital Altrincham, explains:

> *Research has shown regular screen time and excessive screen time can change both the physical structure of the brain such as areas responsible for memory and planning, and how different parts of the brain communicate with each other ... These include thinner areas involved in decision-making, altered connections in regions that control focus, attention and less grey matter in areas crucial for language.*[40]

The result? Research has indicated a sizeable drop in concentration due to excessive screen time.[41] As far back as 2009, evidence showed that students were less likely to absorb what was being taught by the teacher when given access to the internet in the class compared to those without access.[42] Not only this, but just the presence of a smartphone has been proved to cause distraction, even when the owner is not using it.[43] In other words, the concentration problem is not just about young people looking at their phones when they are supposed to be listening. It is much bigger than that.

When I started out in youth work in the early 90s, I measured how well I had been able to communicate by seeing how engaged the young people were. These days, I don't take it to heart when I can see that the young people in front of me are distracted and looking for stimulation. Nor should you. It's okay to request that young people focus on us, but we shouldn't treat a lack of concentration as pure naughtiness.

I recently spoke at an outreach event to nearly 500 unchurched young people who weren't familiar with the church culture of politeness; there was a constant murmur of noise, chatting, and even play-fighting. It was hard work! But rather than getting stressed, I believed in my material and told myself that they would be coming in and out of the talk. Sure enough, when I rounded up, there was a high level of response to the gospel. A casual observer might have assumed that the young people were not listening at all and have been surprised by how much they had assimilated. But the reality was that this Z-A audience was still tracking with the gist of what I was saying. They were taking in less information, for sure, but they were present enough. They hooked in and latched on to the key points that I wanted them to hear.

With this in mind, I would argue that wherever possible, we should push for small groups over large.

Holding young people's attention is a lot easier with smaller groups, especially because you have more flexibility to communicate in different ways, rather than just having one person speaking from the front. I would encourage you to consider plenty of variety and creativity: include discussion, brief sharing of stories, audience participation, video clips, illustrations, and anything else you can think of. Always be authentic and try to be personal whenever you can. These are all the things youth workers have always done, but perhaps they need to be briefer and sharper than before.

## The Power of Reduction

*If you find honey, eat just enough—too much of it, and you will vomit. (Proverbs 25:16)*

The simplicity of Proverbs 25:16 puts teens' nine hours a day of screen time into a framework of excess. Screen time is much like honey. Is it enjoyable? Yes. Is too much of it bad for you? Yes.

There is mounting evidence that cutting back on screen time can lead to improvements in concentration, awareness, listening skills, sleep quality, analytical skills, working memory, and the ability to read body language and social cues. Cognitive function typically bounces back to normal levels when behaviours around digital technology are adjusted. In much of the research I have quoted, the conclusions have been similar: excess is bad; moderation is good. In other words, technology in and of itself is not bad—and the damage caused by excessive use of technology can, in the main, be resolved.

There is power in reduction! If young people have less digital engagement, they will feel healthier, and they will actually get greater pleasure from the limited time they do spend on devices.

It can be socially and emotionally harmful to go from excessive use of digital tech to absolutely nothing. We should be cautious of demanding that of young people, and we should not be surprised by any anxiety that arises because of requests to put away their phones. However, it is completely acceptable to request that phones be put away when we are running any activity, especially when we need young people to be able to focus for things like talks and discussion times. Schools are increasingly implementing such requirements, so many young people are learning to go without screens for longer periods of time.

We can also provide lots of healthy alternative stimulation in whatever clubs or groups we are running for young people, so that phones become less tempting.

But since your time with young people is always going to be very limited, the most important thing you can do is not to set rules about their screen time but simply to open a dialogue on technology and digital engagement and how they feel about it. Try to discuss the "less is more" principle and see how they respond.

Your starting point in such conversations should keep in mind that Gen-Zers generally want to make good, healthy choices, and 75% of Gen Alpha, by 8-10 years old, are already considering the relationship between their tech and their mental health.[44] In fact, two-thirds have stated they would rather go outside more than be on tech, as a means to manage their mental health. You may be aware of a rise in older Gen-Zers ditching smartphones for dumb phones (with no internet capability). Gen Z-A need assistance—the influence of digital technology is a very powerful undercurrent—but many already have a desire and an awareness to work towards greater balance.

### The Bread of Life

When Jesus fed the 5,000, he shortly afterwards made an incredible and, if we're honest, slightly confusing statement:

> *I am the bread of life. Whoever comes to me will never go hungry, and whoever believes in me will never be thirsty. (John 6:35)*

> *Whoever eats this bread will live for ever. This bread is my flesh, which I will give for the life of the world. (v 51)*

Jesus fed hungry people bread and then claimed to *be* bread! He was stating that he provides a satisfaction that goes deep and has eternal ramifications. When we are truly connected to Jesus, our deepest needs are addressed. I don't need to eat sugar when I'm stressed, and I don't need to scroll pointlessly for hours when I have downtime.

It might sound like a cliché, but it's true: Jesus is enough! Yes, we need balance: we need to have fun, exercise, eat, study and so much more. Yet when Jesus is firmly rooted at the centre of our lives, we have enough and can find contentment.

I am a comfort-eater. I didn't think I was until it was pointed out to me in a very stressful meeting where I had demolished most of the muffins that were supposed to be available to everyone! The penny dropped. I realised that I wanted to feel pleasure to solve my stress, and I sought out sugar without even really noticing what I was doing.

Once my sugar issue was pointed out to me, I took it to Jesus and applied discipline. Mostly, I asked Jesus to be present in my stress, because that was the root cause of my challenge. Earlier I quoted a proverb that encourages moderation when eating honey—something that is good except when consumed excessively. But there is a better antidote than simply reducing whatever it is we are addicted to. In Psalm 119, we are reminded of something even better than honey:

> *How sweet are your words to my taste, sweeter than honey to my mouth! (Psalm 119:103)*

That is the hope for young people—not just encouraging them to turn down the frequency of their use of technology but introducing Jesus and turning up the impact he can have on their lives!

So, when an unchurched young person comes to know Christ, don't go soft on discipleship. Set the bar high: encourage them to read their Bible, come to youth group, attend church, share their faith and have a mentor to help with discipleship. They need to replace the sweet honey of digital tech and other unhealthy habits with the nourishing bread of Jesus. Introducing him and setting a new pattern for living will only accelerate the powerful change that happens as young people come under the influence of the Holy Spirit. You could get to help make that happen.

Chapter 8

# Gen Z-A and Social Media

**IF YOU GREW** up before the existence of smartphones, it might amaze you that 82% of young people believe that internet access is just as important as access to clean running water.[45] Why? I'd say that in large part it's because the internet is their means to connect to social media.

In the 17th century, René Descartes said, "I think, therefore I am". The reason why he could be confident that he really did exist was because he was capable of thinking about it! But for today's teens, it might ring truer to say, "My profile exists, therefore I am." To exist without social media would feel like not existing at all.

In other words, social media to teens is not just funny cat reels and trivial life hacks! If you use a search engine to ask why young people use it, two words will most likely surface over and over again: "identity" and "connect". For Gen Z-A, social media is about discovering themselves and one another.

**Creating Identity**

Throughout history, humans have sought to understand the reason for their existence. The psalmist wasn't alone in asking, "What is mankind that you are mindful of them, human beings that you care for them?" (Psalm 8:4). In today's individualistic world, young people are not asking, "Why do we exist?" so much as "Why do *I* exist?" Or, put a different way, "Who am I, and do I matter?" To find their answers, Z-A are turning to social media. This is where they form their identity, image and general persona. Social media is a powerful means to explore and develop who they are and establish their value.

Comparison, peer-led advice, and the pursuit of finding the authentic self leads to hundreds of hours spent scanning profiles, comments, videos, testimonies, posts, debates, likes and dislikes—all helping to form an opinion on who I should be, what I should think and how I should see the world. The question for Z-A has perhaps been edited further, from "Who am I?" to "Who do I *want* to be?" It is less about finding oneself and more about inventing oneself. The selfie goes a long way towards illustrating that. This is the authentic me—after I have adjusted the lighting, taken multiple pictures, selected the one I like the best and placed a filter over it. In truth, it's less about the real me and more about the public me I want you to see. Social media is the place where you first discover and then promote the person you choose to be.

In response, the question for the church and for any youth practitioner has to be: how can we provide an alternative sense of value and purpose—one that goes much deeper than the comparisons and fake personas of social media? How might we provide truer answers to "Who am I" and "Why do I matter?"

We went some way towards answering these questions in chapter 6. We'll look at them again here, alongside growing in our understanding of what young people are experiencing on social media and how we can help them with some of the issues it causes.

## Connecting from Afar

When I was a teenager, I mostly hung out with my friends after school. If I wanted to see someone who lived further away, I had to make an awkward phone call to arrange weekend plans. I say awkward because the phone was in the living room. So although the TV was on in the background, every member of my family quietly listened in to my calls! These days, the TV is still in the living room, and the family still sits around together watching it, but 30% of young people are on their phones while they watch.[46] In other words, private conversations are still happening within the living room, but now it's without eavesdroppers.

In 2017, psychology professor Jean M. Twenge wrote that young people were less interested in leaving the house than they had been previously. In an article for *The Atlantic*, she described the social habits of a 13-year-old named Athena:

> *She spent much of her summer keeping up with friends, but nearly all of it was over text or Snapchat. "I've been on my phone more than I've been with*

> *actual people," she said. "My bed has, like, an imprint of my body."*[47]

Young people are highly connected—yet they are increasingly absent from other actual humans. When Z-A do meet in person, quite often devices are still in their hands, and they spend their time scrolling through social media and direct messaging apps.

In an interview with The Children's Society, 16-year-old Eamon says it far more succinctly than I could:

> *Young people are becoming more unsocial. I believe there is a heavy difference between what our parents and people before us had.*[48]

Since this is the case, we should feel compelled to work hard at creating in-person social engagement for young people. I'll share some thoughts on that a little later on. First, though, we need to see that disconnection is far from being the only challenge that young people are facing in regard to their social-media use.

### The Dark Side of Social Media

The NSPCC website lists a number of challenges and risks for young people connected to social media. These include the possibility of oversharing personal information, the danger of revealing their location to strangers, an unhelpful culture of comparison, and an obsessive need for likes and comments.[49] All very real concerns. But here I want to focus on three even darker sides of social media.

First, sexting. One in five young people have been involved in sending sexual images of themselves to another person via social media or messaging apps. 73% feel regret after sending an intimate image or video of themselves, and 28% of those who have shared such content have either had the image distributed onwards by the recipient or faced threats of it being posted online.[50] It is illegal to take, have or distribute a sexual photo of an under-18, even if it is a photo of yourself; but the offenders very often become the victims.

Second, there is the drug trade, also known as county lines. Young people are often communicated with via social media and then exploited to carry drugs. Along with that goes sexual exploitation of young people, who in many cases send indecent pictures of themselves to unknown sources for cash to feed their own drug habits. That might seem extreme to you, and distant from your community and the people you know; but be aware that a survey in 2021 revealed that 25% of 13-15-year-olds had seen illegal drugs sold online through the most common social-media platforms.[51] Young people in your area are as vulnerable as anyone to this kind of exploitation.

Finally, there is the prolific accessibility of content about violence, rape and suicide. When a 13-year-old signs up to certain popular social-media platforms, it can take a matter of minutes for the algorithms to start sending inappropriate images of death and suicide.[52] If this feels extreme, again let me ground it for you: in a survey of 19,000 17-year-olds taken in 2021, 7% of them admitted to having attempted to end their lives.[53] That's not to say it's all because of social media, but social media will tell them how. Let's not forget the tragic story of Molly Russell and many others like her.

There is a very present danger for young people. While campaigners are working hard, many of us feel powerless to know what to do. Let me encourage you that you can do two simple and practical things. Firstly, pray! Pray with the faith to see light overcome darkness for the young people who are scrolling in isolation in your community. Secondly, talk about what young people are seeing when you engage with them. Listen and ask gentle questions about how that shapes their thinking.

### Fear Steps In

Happily, the majority are not involved in sexual exploitation, the drug trade, or viewing horrible content. But there is one other dark side that does impact every user of social media. In a justice-driven world where tolerance is king, opinions can become dangerous. Views at odds with the majority should expect to encounter cancel culture.

Cancel culture is "a way of behaving in a society or group, especially on social media, in which it is common to completely reject and stop supporting someone because they have said or done something that offends you."[54]

Fear has now stepped into the arena.

People of any age may experience fear around being cancelled, but it is more prevalent among the young. *The Guardian* reported in 2022 that almost half of Gen Z believed people deserved to be cancelled, and more than 1 in 4 young people have "very little tolerance for people with beliefs [they] disagree with".[55]

It is worth pausing for a moment to recognise the irony: tolerance requires acceptance of any viewpoint, *unless* that viewpoint is at odds with what you believe we should be tolerant of.

In an article for *The New York Times*, 17-year-old Neelam explained why she believed in the importance of cancelling people:

> *Cancel culture [is] a way to take away someone's power and call out the individual for being problematic in a situation.*[56]

At the heart of cancel culture is the desire to uphold "tolerance" and disempower opposing views or values. That might sound good—but if you are intolerant or perceived to be intolerant, then you can expect a backlash, and it may not be pretty.

To cancel somebody is to publicly shame an individual, which inevitably impacts their mental health and general wellbeing. Cancelling can lead to bullying, and those who have been cancelled are more likely to experience loneliness, anxiety and depression.[57] Research on the brains of adolescents has revealed that social rejection can cause actual pain.[58] So the impact of being cancelled is no small thing for a young person.

As young people watch just how brutal public shaming can get, they start to fear that they, too, could be cancelled. Writing on the website Verywell Mind, Lindsey Toler explains that young bystanders "become overwhelmed with anxiety that people will turn on them if they fully express themselves. This can cause them to keep their thoughts bottled up instead of talking about and working through their opinions and emotions."[59]

Gen Alpha and, to some degree, Gen Z, depending on their proximity to Alpha, are increasingly conflict-averse (unless they have the reassurance of being backed by the crowd and have no fear of backlash). I was recently chatting to a group of lads about injustice. I asked, "If you saw a young kid being bullied at school, would you step in?" Every one of the boys said no. I was surprised and asked why. The answer was simple: "In case the teachers think I was involved and I get the blame for it." I then provided other examples: what if someone held a view you just couldn't accept? I was greeted with silence. I pushed harder, only to discover this group of lads would all hold back. "What's the point?!" It seems that the result of cancel culture, in some cases, is a pendulum swing in the other direction: clear injustices are going unchallenged by young people who are afraid of the possible consequences of going against the crowd.

Nobody wants to be cancelled. Nobody wants to be cyberbullied. Nobody wants to be addicted to a device, and nobody wants to become so superficial that their entire identity is caught up in the likes and approvals of people online. And yet this is the reality for so many members of Gen Z-A.

## Shame and Grace

Etched in my mind as I write is the latest viral social-media moment. A man and a woman, arms wrapped around each other as they sway to the music at a

Coldplay concert, quickly hide their faces and jump apart when they realise the camera has zoomed in on them. Something is clearly not right. Chris Martin, Coldplay's lead singer, speculates from the stage that they are either having an affair or are very shy.

It didn't take long for the internet to flood with memes and ridicule the two individuals—who, it turned out, were indeed having an affair. The man, a high-profile CEO, resigned from his job within days of the images going viral.

Cancel culture isn't the only way in which public shaming and brutal bullying are experienced through the internet. When a young person publicly does something embarrassing, gone are the days of being teased on the school bus; now, people create a meme about them and let the world know just how much of a fool they have been. The mockery and bullying is next level.

Jesus had a different approach. When the Pharisees sought to test Jesus by publicly shaming a woman who was having an affair, Jesus didn't focus on her sin but on their hypocrisy. As they explained that the law stipulates that she should be stoned to death, Jesus affirmed the law with a caveat:

> *Let any one of you who is without sin be the first to throw a stone at her. (John 8:7)*

There will be many moments when young people who are connected with your activities are being called out and shamed for something or other. Our response should be to focus on the fallibility of all of us rather than the mistakes of one individual—even as we encourage those who have acted sinfully to stop what they are doing and choose a better path.

### The Golden Rule

It might appear odd for me to say this, but I don't believe all social media is bad. I don't think that for a moment! In fact, the surge in 18-24-year-olds attending church could in part be to do with social media. I simply recognise that there is a brutality to social media for young people. What starts off as self-expression or self-reflection too often becomes comparison and poor self-esteem. What starts off as experimenting with different viewpoints ends up in public rejection and shaming. What starts off as a private joke becomes widespread, hateful bullying.

But imagine if we could positively change all of that by presenting powerful alternatives!

> *Finally, brothers and sisters, whatever is true, whatever is noble, whatever is right, whatever is pure, whatever is lovely, whatever is admirable—if anything is excellent or praiseworthy—think about such things.*
>
> *(Philippians 4:8)*

If what I view, what I post and what I respond to can pass the Philippians 4:8 test, then I am not going to create so many problems for myself with the way I feel about myself, the way I see others and the way I view the world and my place within it.

Then there's Jesus' golden rule:

> *Do to others what you would have them do to you.*
>
> *(Matthew 7:12)*

If we could help this generation understand just this one idea, we would start to transform online behaviour. These words bring freedom! Could the rule be any simpler? Yet could it be any more powerful? If you seek to be liked, respected, and generally valued, then do the same to everyone else. Approaching everything through that lens will result in different outcomes from the current minefield of social media today.

## The Power of Moving Offline

We are social beings. We are designed to connect in person, to learn how to effectively communicate, to talk through problems and address relational tensions, to understand social cues, to enjoy making others happy and to feel distressed when we cause hurt. Digital communication does not allow for the clarity brought by body language and tone of voice. People lack empathy from afar and cannot see the pain that they may be inflicting when every interaction takes place through a device.

So, what can we do as Christian adults? There are many opportunities. You might become an advocate for online safety; you might read up on online safeguarding guidelines and find out what you can do to provide support to young people in your area, helping them better understand the dangers and opportunities they face online. You might talk to young people you know about how to reflect a message of positivity on social media.

But all of us can take the simple step of helping teens to go back to basics. Create safe spaces where young people are able to interact in person and discover how to positively build healthy relationships. We can also speak truth, positivity and value over the young people we interact with. For those in places of distress, hurt and pain, we can listen and speak truth and hope. We can prove ourselves to be trustworthy so that young people feel safe telling us about online bullying or other ways in which they are vulnerable or at risk—imagine how profoundly important such a moment could be for a young person! Finally, we can pray that God would come through and bring relief to those struggling. All of this will have a far greater and longer-lasting impact than simply telling young people to stop using social media for good.

You get to be an agent of change! Ultimately, you are Christ's ambassador to young lives. That is a powerful opportunity.

Chapter 9

# Gen Z-A and Mental Health

**AT JUST 16** I was hospitalised for depression and anxiety.

I was admitted on New Year's Eve, and was placed on observation, which meant bars on the window and someone stationed outside my room or with me 24/7. I was in a bad way. When family came to visit, I just wished they hadn't—not because I didn't want to see them but because I was embarrassed about being "weak". My grandma had told me that as she drove me to the hospital, "You need to be stronger. Only you can snap yourself out of it." The problem was, I couldn't!

It was shortly after being discharged from hospital that I found faith in Jesus. Now the family oddball had become a "religious nut job"! Apparently, religion was my crutch for dealing with my "mental breakdown". At family gatherings, I was given a wide berth. I was told it was all just a fad and I would come right in the end.

I'm not sure I would be treated the same way if I were a young person being hospitalised for depression today. Previous generations didn't like to talk about mental health, but now it has become an acceptable subject. However, it is a myth to say that the rise in depression and anxiety among today's young people is simply down to the fact that mental health is less of a taboo than it used to be. The mentally unwell have always been among us, it's true; but there is now a disproportionate rise in poor mental health, especially among young people.

> *Between 2017 and 2023, rates of probable mental disorder increased from around 1 in 8 young people aged 8-16 to more than 1 in 6. For those aged 17-19, rates increased from 1 in 10 to 1 in 4.*[60]

That adds up to about 1 in 5 young people in the UK aged between 8 and 25 who had a probable mental disorder in 2023.[61] Meanwhile, before the pandemic, the American Psychological Association noted a 40% rise across ten years of feelings of persistent sadness and hopelessness as well as suicidal thoughts and behaviour among young people.[62]

Something has rocked the mental health of Gen Z-A!

### Changes in Parenting

The social psychologist Jonathan Haidt, in his heavily researched book *The Anxious Generation*, argues that there are two major sources of today's mental-health problems among Gen Z-A. One is the rise of digital tech and the challenges associated with it—which we've discussed in the previous two chapters. The other is overprotective parenting.

The big shift in modern parenting occurred with Gen-Xers (those born between 1965 and 1980). While Boomer parents tended to have a relatively authoritarian discipline style, pushing high educational standards and being comparatively absent from their children's lives, Gen X sought to correct that approach and protect their children more. That might sound good, but based on numerous pieces of research (especially that undertaken by Jonathan Haidt), overprotective parenting isn't coming out entirely smelling of roses. It seems that focusing on protecting our children has actually led to higher rates of anxiety and difficulties in regulating emotions.

In 1954, psychologist Julian Rotter coined the term Locus of Control (LOC). In essence, LOC is about an individual's confidence or belief about how much control they have over their lives. People with low-level LOC seem to have greater anxiety and depression. Peter Gray believes that when a child develops their ability to make decisions and solve problems through play, the result is a strong internal LOC. But modern children lack opportunities to play and learn independently. Just a few decades ago, children as young as five or six would play out of sight of their parents and thus learn independence. Such learning shaped how much control an individual personally believed they had over their life at a later stage—resulting in a lower prevalence of anxiety and depression.[63]

One thing we need to consider in our youth work, then, is how we can create environments where young people can take appropriate risks and make decisions for themselves—while, yes, remaining within acceptable and safe boundaries! How might we instil confidence and independence in a way that doesn't induce anxiety for them but builds a bank of evidence to support confidence? If our goal is to introduce young people to "life to the full" in Jesus, then that includes helping to build their emotional resilience and self-confidence.

## Responding to Anxiety

It was 1997, I was leading an event for 300 young people, and one teenage girl was struggling to breathe. At the time, the solution was a brown paper bag and the instruction to breathe slowly into it. So that's what we gave her. The paramedics arrived. It turned out she wasn't asthmatic, as we had assumed, but was having a panic attack. I had heard about such a thing but until that point I had never seen it.

These days, at almost every large gathering of young people I attend, someone somewhere is likely to have a panic attack. It has become so common and normal. Whether someone is struggling to regulate their breathing or is shaking, sweating or in an overly upset state, a seasoned youth leader will spot the signs.

There is plenty of advice online about how to help someone who is having a panic attack. The main thing to know is that an anxiety attack is very real; it isn't a sulk, and it is not being overhyped. It is a real bodily reaction to fear—though the person may not even be aware of where that fear comes from. We need to help them to see that they are safe.

In the moment, provide gentle reassurance with a

focus on deep regulated breathing, and encourage the individual that the attack will pass. Once the panic has subsided, ask what is concerning the young person. It may be something that can be talked through, such as an exam or a relationship, or it may be a more general sense of guilt and shame. You do not have to have all the answers to their problems—but awareness and sensitivity on their own will go a long way in helping young people deal with anxiety. If there seems to be a complex or serious cause of the panic, you will need to move sensitively into safeguarding mode and perhaps signpost them to a mental-health practitioner who has the experience to help them.

The worst thing we can do is to try to fix people by getting into things we are not qualified for or just giving bad advice. The next worst thing we can do is ignore it, as if it's just a toddler tantrum. But what's the *best* thing we can do to help young people with their anxiety? Of course, it is to point them to Jesus.

### Come to Me

Mental health is very complex and covers a wide range of subjects, so I am aware there is no "one size fits all". I am also aware that religion itself can be a trigger for some people. With that in mind, I make the following comments carefully.

> *Come to me, all you who are weary and burdened, and I will give you rest. (Matthew 11:28)*

This invitation to bring our anxiety to Jesus is offered to anyone and everyone. It doesn't mean the fear or sadness will disappear, but it does mean that we can bring it to him, and he will sit with us in it. This is an invitation and not a command; Jesus won't be mad or offended if we are too overwhelmed to take it up. His invitation remains.

When my daughter, Molly, was in her first year at university, she had a friend who struggled with poor mental health. Let's call him Adrian for this account. Adrian would often be missing from his studies for large chunks of time, staying in his room for days on end with just his smart device. On one particular Saturday, around late morning, Molly reached out to Adrian to discover that he was still in his bed and had no plans to get out of it for the rest of the weekend. Molly's response was direct and firm but kind. "Adrian, I need you to get out of bed, take a shower, brush your teeth, get dressed and have breakfast. You then need to meet me in 30 minutes. We are going to look at something the Bible has to say."

Adrian wasn't a Christian—he hadn't even shown any interest in Molly's faith—but he responded to her very practical instructions. He got up, showered, brushed his teeth, got dressed and had some food. Slightly longer than 30 minutes later, he met with Molly. They sat down, and she opened the Bible and read Genesis 16 and the account of Hagar. That might have seemed a little odd, but she hovered over verse 13:

*You are the God who sees me.*

"Adrian," Molly said, "you are not invisible to God. He sees you, and he knows you. Furthermore he invites you to know him. You don't need to feel alone."

For Adrian, understanding that God sees him was the first step in discovery. Anxiety had caused him to feel alone. It had prompted him to withdraw from people, making his isolation more real and more profound. But when Adrian realised that he was not alone after all, he was able to take a step forward.

In the 2025 study *The Quiet Revival*, it was highlighted that those between 18 and 34 who are Christians (to be precise, those who attend church, pray and read their Bibles) are happier with their life and are less likely to feel anxious or depressed compared to those who are unchurched.[64] The same level of data, as far as I am aware, is not available for under-18s—but what's clear is that faith in Jesus and a connection to a Christian community make a clear difference in one's wellbeing and emotional outlook. That's not to say Christian young people do not face considerable mental-health challenges, but following Jesus makes a difference. That should be no surprise to us!

When an unchurched parent asked me, "What have you done to my son?" I felt a sense of fear! When Tom started coming to our church youth activities, he had consistently been the last to walk through the door; he would always sit at the back and seemed the least engaged. Tom definitely had an edge; there was some deep stuff going on with him. But in time, he became more engaged and eventually decided to follow Jesus. It was shortly after that that the question came: "What have you done to my son?"

"What do you mean?" I asked cautiously.

"Tom is a different boy," came the enthusiastic reply.

"He's polite and calm and does things the first time I ask him. He even helps around the house. Whatever you are doing, keep doing it!"

Let's be clear, we didn't do that to Tom! Rather, he had experienced Jesus, and Jesus had fulfilled his promise to give him rest—to heal the broken-hearted, set the captives free and release the oppressed (Luke 4:18).

When Jesus informed the disciples that he would be leaving them, he comforted them with these words:

> *Peace I leave with you; my peace I give you ... Do not let your hearts be troubled and do not be afraid.*
> *(John 14:27)*

This isn't a soundbite but a promise. Our role is to help young people discover Jesus and experience the peace that can overcome fear.

### A Whole-Life Gospel

There has been a pattern that we at Youth for Christ have noticed for some time when it comes to young people and their interest in faith. Where there is growth, it is often connected to experience. There is no doubt in my mind that young people are less interested in facts and intellectual proof and more interested in experience and transformation. When they are exploring faith, they want to know whether it works and what difference it makes. That fits, since Jesus both declared and demonstrated the good news. The gospel is both theoretical and practical!

If we only declare the good news to young people using words and concepts, we are missing an opportunity.

Let's not just talk at teenagers—let's think about their mental, physical and social growth, and how the spiritual reality of the gospel can impact and connect with those things. Let's invite them into something experiential, not just theoretical.

That means talking through with them the issues they care about—moral or theological—in group discussions or pairs. It means developing real relationships of care and trust. It means engaging with them about technology and social media, and thinking through how to create spaces where they can be free from the more negative effects of those things. It means working to make prayer feel real—you might encourage young people to hold and use a printed Bible rather than their phone, or bring in other simple physical acts like lighting a candle, smelling incense, grabbing a holding cross, kneeling in silence or singing.

Luke 2:52 tells us that Jesus, as a young person, grew "in wisdom and stature, and in favour with God and man". In other words, he grew mentally, physically, spiritually and socially. If we can address all four of these key areas, we will connect with young people's entire selves in the brief time they are with us. We will invite them into the truly full life that Jesus longs for them to have.

# 4

# Reaching Out

Chapter 10

# Going into the Community

**EVERY TUESDAY EVENING,** Analice and two other volunteers from a church in London go out onto the streets armed with hot chocolate, Jaffa cakes and identical hoodies that say "youth worker" on the back. The hoodies alone create conversations, and the chocolate is always a gathering point. The first time the team approached a cluster of teenagers, it seemed a little daunting—but as soon as they explained that they were volunteer youth workers from a local church and they just wanted to say hi, connect and find out how the young people were doing, the offer of hot chocolate was accepted, and conversations flowed. Now, every Tuesday, Analice and her team talk with local teens about school, friendships and of course the weather! Fifty percent of the time, the conversations move to God. While most of the young people have no church connections, they often want to talk about faith, spirituality and meaning.

Analice is running informal, no-commitment discipleship meetings in the park with a group of young people that she meets week on week, and they remain happy to talk to her. Those young people wouldn't consider that they are having church time. But they are connecting, discussing things about God, eating and drinking and, when the opportunity arises, even praying—whether it be about an exam, problems at home or a sickness. This isn't exactly church, but it isn't a million miles away from it either. Analice is taking small steps with them towards a much bigger picture.

What Analice does each week is known as "detached work". This simply means engaging with young people "where they are at", providing youth work in non-formal environments in the community where young people are located. You are most likely familiar with the term "outreach"; detached work is very similar but ever so slightly different. Outreach goes out to people in the community to bring them back in. For example, youth workers going to young people in the park to invite them to a church youth centre. Detached work is going to where young people are and staying with them. I want to help you explore both options in this chapter.

## Mapping Your Community

In 2016, Youth for Christ published some research on the behaviour of 11-18-year-olds. It revealed that the most popular thing to do was hang out with friends outside or (slightly less popular) in their homes. Perhaps most interestingly, 24% of young people said they connected with their mates online.[65] In 2025, we asked the same questions again. A staggering 63% mainly connected with their friends via social media and 57% through online gaming. As for connecting in person, 58% said they hung out with their friends in their home, 46% mentioned parks, 36% public spaces, 29% sports clubs, 19% on the street, 18% in a youth group or club and 7% skate parks.[66]

In other words, habits have changed, but not totally. While young people are spending more time behind screens and indoors, they *are* still out in the community, whether it be in the park, the shops or fast-food outlets, or just hanging out on the street.

So where are the young people hanging out in your community?

In order to be really informed, I want to encourage you to do a basic community mapping assessment:

- Either get in your car and drive around the area or, if you have more time, walk the streets. Note what you see and, in particular, where you see young people.

- Get a local map or print a screenshot of an online map. Highlight the following: parks, youth clubs and centres, leisure centres, shopping centres, schools, the high street, fast-food places, and any cinemas and other entertainment locations. Also highlight your church.

- This step will take a little bit of work, and you will need others to help you do it. Visit the main places you have identified on the map within a one- or two-mile radius of your church. Do it at multiple times; include straight after school and between 6 and 8 p.m. on weeknights, as well as a daytime and an evening slot on a weekend. It may be helpful to wear a high-vis jacket and bring ID (you should definitely do this once you start the work itself); be aware that you may raise suspicion.

- On your map, shade in with a pencil the places where young people's footfall and congregating happen. (Use light shading for fewer instances of young people gathering and darker shading for more.) Include now your notes from when you patrolled the entire area in step one. This will start to give you a strong idea of where young people are.

With the information you have gathered, start to consider how you could connect with unchurched young people in the community. Where are they, and what could you offer them? Pray about it. (Go back to my suggestions in chapter 3!) Here are some ideas to get you started:

- Go out on foot in a small team to local parks and other places, and start conversations.
- Set up a stall in a market or town centre, offering free Bibles or a conversation or prayer. Or simply serve free drinks and snacks and say that you are from the local church and want to get to know local young people.
- Stand in a shopping centre offering a questionnaire to people about their relationship with God or religion.
- Run an event in a local community centre.
- Walk around the town praying together and see what happens.

- Run a regular drop-in club in your church or in a community centre, and go out to invite young people to it. Provide games and comfy seats, and offer a non-confrontational opportunity to engage with who God is in some way.
- Start a sports club, cooking club, homework club or other regular event.

To aid your thinking, it can also be really helpful to contact the local police (ask to speak to a Police Community Support Officer) or the local council (request a meeting with the Council Community Development Officer). Explain who you are and that you are seeking to provide support for young people in the local area. Ask them for their insights into where young people congregate and what they are seeing and hearing.

That might seem daunting, but my expectation is that the local authorities will greatly welcome your involvement—even when they hear that you are from the church and that you want to share your faith. Between 2011 and 2021, there was a reduction of over 50% in local-authority spending on youth provision. The result has been spikes in shoplifting, weapons-related incidents and young offenders' reoffending.[67] There is a direct correlation between a lack of youth provision and young people getting into trouble! Your presence will help change the statistics for the better; the authorities know that and are likely to welcome your involvement.

**Jade's Story**

I would like to tell you about a young man named Jade and what came from his encounter with two Christian outreach workers.

Jade had known dysfunction in his life. Things were messy at home, so he spent more time out than in. He drank and hung out with his mates. When he was approached by a couple of adults in high-vis jackets calling themselves youth workers, Jade was a little uncertain as to who they were and what they wanted. It was cold and wet, and the youth workers told them about a drop-in centre. Jade had heard of it, and because it was cold and wet, he agreed to go. The club was packed—there were at least 80-100 young people. Jade saw a bunch of zones with different activities—video gaming, table tennis, air hockey, craft and, intriguingly, a spiritual room. There were rules regarding this room. You could only go in if you promised to be quiet and respectful. It had a queue! It turned out that this room was the most popular zone. Jade was curious.

When his turn came to enter the spiritual room, Jade went in, wondering if some mystic would be in there with tarot cards or a crystal ball. The room was dimly lit and filled with cushions; there were a couple of leaders and a few other teens, all quiet. Jade sat down at a table in the middle of the room. There was an open book—the Bible—and a few handwritten cards. It was incredibly quiet in this room, especially given the noise outside. No one was talking.

Jade picked up a card that asked, "If you could ask God to do anything for you right now, what would you ask?"

The question stunned him. Ten minutes before, he had been drinking a can of beer. Now he was sitting in a softly lit, comfortable room. He was struck by how peaceful he felt. Maybe the alcohol was kicking in.

"What would I ask him to do?" He had no idea.

He picked up another card; it was some kind of quote.

*Peace I leave with you; my peace I give you. I do not give to you as the world gives. Do not let your hearts be troubled and do not be afraid. (John 14:27)*

He read the quote again and again.

Jade was in there for more than an hour. He didn't notice all the other people coming and going. He just couldn't leave.

Jade became a frequent attendee of the drop-in club. Over time, he discovered that it was run by a church. He ended up joining the church youth group and learning more about Jesus. Eventually, Jade decided to follow Jesus for himself.

### Go and Make Disciples

Don't miss the steps in Jade's journey. It started with two youth workers inviting him to attend a drop-in club, which resulted in some kind of "spiritual moment", which transitioned into him joining the youth group and eventually hearing enough about Jesus that he knew he wanted him in his life. It was gradual. And for Jade to come in, the first step was people from the church going out.

In exactly the same way, in order to turn around the life of the woman at the well, Jesus had to go to

Samaria, meet her on her own turf and talk about her life. And what was the result of that encounter? Not only the woman herself but many others came to faith:

> *Many of the Samaritans from that town believed in him because of the woman's testimony, "He told me everything I've ever done." (John 4:39)*

Jesus met with strangers where they were, in their community. He expected the same of the disciples:

> *Calling the Twelve to him, he began to send them out two by two. (Mark 6:7)*

And he asks the same of us.

> *Therefore go and make disciples of all nations.*
> *(Matthew 28:19)*

Wait, that says "nations"! Yes. But it starts local. Jesus' first followers started in Jerusalem, then went to all Judea and Samaria, and eventually reached the ends of the earth (Acts 1:8). Our outreach in local places is what ends up having a global outcome.

### Starting a Club

When I visited Dorset Youth for Christ, I was told that their cooking club had 120 young people attending it. It ran once a week and started as a simple safe space for a few teenagers as something to do after school. It started very small but grew exponentially, requiring more support and resources. When I asked Aaron, the centre director, why it had grown so much, he told me that he'd asked the same question of the young people.

Their response was universal: this was the only time they were guaranteed food. Dorset has pockets of deprivation, but it's hardly the poster location for poverty—yet food poverty was what these young people were experiencing.

The answers Aaron received stirred him into action. Lobbying both the council and churches, he established a food bank. When a young person attends the club now, they are provided with a hot dog as soon as they walk through the door. They then cook and can take home what they have made, but that's not all; they are also given a box to help feed their entire family for the week. What an amazing starting point for conversations about faith!

Let's imagine you decide to run an outreach club similar to the one in Dorset. My advice is to start small—don't overcomplicate it. For example, you might want to offer a homework club on a Wednesday afternoon right after school. Does your church have a hall or warm space? Access to the internet will help, as will having tables and chairs. You will need a few volunteers (with DBS checks), and if you have a retired or current teacher available, all the better. Don't just make it about homework; offer hot chocolate, soft drinks and cake. There is probably someone in your church who loves to bake. This is all you need.

How do you run it? For the majority of the time, make the club purely a study space. Then, for the last 15-30 minutes, consider starting some activities. One or two cringe-free icebreaker games can be helpful. Try starting a discussion with a topical question like "In the news today, a report came out about mobile phone addiction. What do you think it would mean to have an addiction to a mobile phone?" The aim is not to teach the young people anything but simply to stir up conversation. As the weeks go on, start to introduce God into these discussions.

Nothing about the club needs to be complicated. Advertise it to any young people you already have in your church and encourage them to bring friends. If you don't have young people at your church, then ask a local school if you can run the club in a classroom straight after the bell for home has gone. The school will most likely be happy to give a room free of charge and to promote the club for you.

### The Thing You Can Excel At

There are plenty of things you can do in detached work and outreach. Getting to know young people, befriending them and building relationships; providing advice and information or mentoring; doing sport or other activities; being a presence on the street and deterring violence—all these are great goals and can make a real difference. These are all things your church can do, and do well, I am sure.

However, there is one thing you can excel at that is unique to you as a church and can't be done by secular youth workers: you can make disciples, just as Analice does every week, and just as Jade experienced after he turned up to the drop-in club. Whether on the street or through an organised club, connecting with young people and nurturing a relationship over time opens the opportunity to journey alongside them towards Jesus.

After all, discipleship isn't a formal class! Yes, it can involve that, but at its core, discipleship is learning the ways of Jesus through living life with people. If you have proximity to young people and you are seeking to meet a need—if you are doing things "with" young people rather than "to" young people—then deeper conversations will surface soon enough. This generation values personal connections over the role of an institution, so be yourself and show that you care. That's all you need to do.

## A Checklist

Here are a few practical/legal things you will need to consider as you start detached or outreach work:

- Run DBS checks and take up references for all volunteers. People need to know you are safe and trustworthy.
- Conduct safeguarding training for all volunteers.
- Use ID badges and/or high-vis jackets, or another clearly identifiable uniform, to mark out who the official volunteers are.
- Explore whether you need public liability insurance if you are putting on an event.
- Conduct a risk assessment.
- Consider the ratios of adults to under-18s. For 13-18s, the NSPCC recommends one adult for every ten children as a minimum. But think in terms of one adult to every three or four children if you can.

Chapter 11

# Working with Schools

**"WE DON'T DO** God."

These were the words of Tony Blair's press secretary, Alastair Campbell, regarding the politics of the then British Prime Minister. Ironically, a few years later, Campbell had to admit, "Well, he [Blair] does do God, umm, in quite a big way."

For me, those two statements capture the UK school system perfectly. It doesn't do God, and yet it kind of does do God in quite a big way!

Of course, attitudes towards faith among those in positions of influence within school systems range considerably—there are staunch atheists, indifferent agnostics, committed Christians and practising Muslims leading schools up and down the UK. Such gatekeepers can open or close doors to Christian work, based on where they sit on the spectrum of belief.

Yet even an atheist headteacher who has no desire to promote religious faith is faced with a moral dilemma: to obey or disobey the law. As it currently stands, the law in England, Wales and Northern Ireland requires a daily act of collective worship for pupils.[68] (In Scotland, it is not required.)

The government guidance doesn't just provide a one-line requirement but a detailed breakdown of what the requirement means and what is expected. For example, "daily" means daily and "worship" means "wholly or mainly of a broadly Christian character".[69] While parents can opt their children out, and legal opposition has been lingering for years, there is no escaping the fact that schools (at the time of writing, and with the exception of non-Christian faith schools) are expected to gather pupils for worship and teaching of the Christian faith.

But while "doing God" is the law for schools, many certainly do not provide daily acts of collective Christian (or any) worship, and a growing number do not do it at all. While this is partly as a result of gatekeepers who actively avoid collective worship, I would suggest that the vast majority are simply under-resourced and uncertain about how to do it. This is where you come in!

### Mutually Beneficial

Consider contacting the local schools within your area. Explain that you are from the local church and would like to arrange a meeting to talk about any ways your church can be of help to the school. It might surprise you that I want to encourage you not to go straight in with the God route. They immediately know of the God connection by your reference to the church. Be aware that the school has many needs, and if they don't know you, then they have every right to be suspicious of you and what you might say or do. How do they know you aren't an extremist or a threat to young people's wellbeing? Teachers are required to think in those ways now.

You are probably longing to connect with local schools in order to meaningfully engage with young people and share Jesus straight off the bat. But consider a different lens—one of being a valued partner to the school. If you can get to the point where you can be considered an extension of their team, where trust is high and confidence in who you are is raised, you will most likely find that the school becomes more than happy to endorse your out-of-school activities or let you lead a school assembly. At that point, you have a mutually beneficial relationship.

So what might that look like?

Carrie is the town's Christian youth worker. She has built a strong relationship with a local school by providing mentoring support, particularly for vulnerable and neurodiverse children who need extra assistance. While she isn't a trained teacher, she functions in many ways as a support staff member—and the school values her contribution highly.

Carrie is not there to share Jesus as such, but her presence has begun to change perceptions of faith in the school environment. Imagine if this kind of quiet, consistent service became more common. Over time, a deeper relationship between schools and local Christian communities could lead to new opportunities for practical support and witness.

To "do God", we may first need to "show God"—living out Jesus' words: "Even the Son of Man did not come to be served, but to serve" (Mark 10:48). That might look like listening to children read, offering mentoring, or helping run a breakfast club. Simple acts of service often open unexpected doors for deeper impact.

When Dave, a youth worker, asked his local school how he might be able to help them, they asked if he could drive. The next thing he knew, he had signed up to pick up a pupil every day from his house. The boy had a high truancy rate, his parents weren't motivated to get him to school, and he was falling through the system. Now, every weekday, Dave drives to the boy's house, picks him up and takes him to school.

When another pupil tragically died and the school was in crisis, they turned to Dave and asked if he could provide pastoral support. Dave had become a valued, trusted member of the school's extended team, who also happened to be a pastor.

Relational connectivity matters; it builds trust and confidence. Carrie and Dave continue to provide mentoring and driving, but they also both lead assemblies on a regular basis, ticking the schools' box for collective worship. It's a win-win for everyone!

So what might you do? Here are some non-faith-based activities that your local schools may appreciate help with:

- Classroom support
- SEN (Special Educational Needs) support
- Hearing children read

- Help or training on a specialist subject or skill
- Mentoring or counselling
- Supporting with day trips or residential trips
- Supervising children in the playground
- Breakfast clubs or after-school clubs
- Lunchtime activity clubs
- Assisting with school plays or productions
- Driving children

Do you think any of those could suit you or others in your church? Try reaching out to a local school and see.

**Religious Education**

Let's get back to the law. Religious education (predominantly Christian) must be included within the school system. However, tensions are once again at play. Here is OFSTED's fairly damning report on religious education in the UK in 2023:

> *RE in schools is generally of poor quality. Although it is a statutory subject, schools often consider RE as an afterthought. As a subject on the curriculum, it is under-valued. RE is a complex subject, and the lack of clarity and support from government makes schools' job harder. Some schools steer through these challenges well, but most do not ... too often, schools do not teach topics in the RE curriculum deeply enough for pupils to develop a substantial understanding of the subject matter.*[70]

Once again, you can be a real help. It's unlikely you will become an RE teacher—though Youth for Christ staff are often seconded to a school team to teach RE, and the same might be the case for you if you have the time, desire and knowledge. But here is where you can most likely help: within the curriculum is a desire for pupils to hear about people's lived experience of religious faith. In other words, schools want people of faith to come in and talk about it! That is something you can offer.

Would your local school welcome someone from the church coming in to speak at an assembly once a month? Perhaps they would like some interviewees for an RE lesson. Could you welcome a year group on a trip to visit your church building and hear about what goes on there? Could you suggest setting up a Christian Union or other simple club at lunchtime or after school? There are plenty of options if you will pray and make yourself available.

**Trust and Opportunities**

Helen and her local Youth for Christ team were providing mentoring and mental-health support for the pupils in a school. One day the school principal asked to see Helen.

"Having you guys in our school makes such a difference to the culture. What can we do in return for you?"

Helen thought for a moment and asked if she could run a lunch club offering the opportunity for young people to discover the Bible for themselves.

The plan was very simple: place a few Bibles on tables and invite the students to explore them and ask questions. It seemed pretty basic. But to my surprise, the club was packed week after week. They came because they liked Helen and the relationship she had already built with them, but they stuck around for a totally different reason. What surprised me the most was that at the end of the lunch club, the students would take out their phones and start photographing the pages of the Bible. When Helen asked why they were taking pictures, the reply was simple: "We don't have Bibles at home; we aren't religious. But when we come here and read these verses, it makes us feel peaceful. We want to be able to look at them when we are at home!"

To my shame and delight, I had to be reminded of the power of God at work through his word. The Bible was laid bare, and in its simplicity it captured unchurched young people. They felt its power!

I shouldn't have been surprised—after all, doesn't God tell us in Isaiah 55:

> *As the rain and the snow come down from heaven,*
> *and do not return to it without watering the earth*
> *and making it bud and flourish, so that it yields seed*
> *for the sower and bread for the eater, so is my word*
> *that goes out from my mouth: it will not return to me*
> *empty, but will accomplish what I desire and achieve*
> *the purpose for which I sent it. (Isaiah 55:10-11)*

We ended up supplying youth Bibles for every single student who came, with the permission of the school, so that no one had to take pictures anymore; they all had their very own copy.

The school welcomed the contribution of the extra-curricular Bible lunch club because they trusted Helen.

When genuine trust is established with a school, regardless of the gatekeepers' own beliefs, there is very often an openness to what else you might offer.

### One Out of Ten

As you journey with young people in a school setting, it might not seem like much, but you can provide real help to some who are in serious need. School can be a mixed bag; lots of young people love it, but many loathe it. When people are struggling with their mental health or become marginalised or victims of bullying, they need someone who brings sunlight: one person who can make a difference to how they feel, even if it doesn't solve all their problems. You could be that person for someone in school.

If that doesn't seem like enough—if you're thinking, "But what I really want is to share Jesus, and what if I never get to do that?"—consider the story of the ten lepers.

> *Now on his way to Jerusalem, Jesus travelled along the border between Samaria and Galilee. As he was going into a village, ten men who had leprosy met him. They stood at a distance and called out in a loud voice, "Jesus, Master, have pity on us!"*
>
> *When he saw them, he said, "Go, show yourselves to the priests." And as they went, they were cleansed.*
>
> *One of them, when he saw he was healed, came back, praising God in a loud voice. He threw himself at Jesus' feet and thanked him—and he was a Samaritan.*
>
> *(Luke 17:11-16)*

There are ten people in desperate need in that story. To the casual observer, Jesus doesn't do anything other than send them off. Yet on the journey, they are healed.

For nine out of ten of the lepers, that's where it ends. A great outcome—their lives are changed! But for the tenth, there is something even better. He comes back, praises God and worships Jesus.

You may journey with hundreds or even thousands of young people across the schools in your area. To help them deal with the challenges in life is a major win and privilege—and for nine out of ten, that's where it will end, at least for now. You have helped them and contributed in a meaningful way to the school. But perhaps the tenth young person may go on to consider faith and, specifically, Jesus. Just like that one leper.

I remember going to a McDonald's drive-thru once when I lived and worked in London. I placed my order and drove to the pay window. "Hello, sir, how are you?" came an enthusiastic voice. Surprised, I looked to see who was talking to me, but I didn't recognise her. "You used to come into my school and talk about God!" she said. I smiled, wondering how she felt about that. "I loved it when you did," she told me. "I can remember what you talked about! It made sense to me!"

I can't remember what I ordered that day, but I can remember how that interaction made me feel. Much of the time we won't even know what impact we have had on young people, in schools or anywhere else. But we should pray that, just as with the lepers, our efforts to make a difference to teens' lives will result in a harvest of salvation for some.

Let me leave you with one last reflection as we come to the close of the chapter. In our research in 2025, we discovered that for 46% of young people in the UK, the only time they ever hear about Christianity is in a religious education lesson. Almost half of all young people only learn about God in school.

I hope you will get involved!

Chapter 12

# Welcoming at Church

**CHURCH ATTENDANCE DATA** has changed rapidly. In 2018, a poll of churches across the UK and Ireland revealed that two-thirds of churches had fewer than five children.[71] Yet when a group of 900 churches were tracked by the Church of England over five years (2013–2018), 44% saw growth in youth ministry![72]

In 2020, only 4% of young people in the UK were attending church.[73] Now that number has doubled to around 8%.[74] It's really encouraging, but those shoots are not seen everywhere. Growth is uneven and depends heavily on denomination, theology and church culture.

The question is: how can your church be one of the ones that sees growth? That's what I've been hoping to answer throughout this book. Hopefully by now you are feeling much better equipped with an understanding of how you can reach out to unchurched young people with the gospel.

In this chapter we'll focus specifically on what it looks like to make young people welcome once they make it through the doors of church—particularly, how to run a youth group session that takes account of unchurched teens.

We have to recognise that there are some distinct differences between how much experience teens have of church. There are young people who have never been part of church; young people raised in church-attending homes who do not own any faith for themselves; and young people who have made decisions to follow Jesus and own their faith, regardless of whether they attend with their family or not. There are unchurched young people who have no interest in faith or understanding and are cold or neutral, and unchurched young people who have turned up either out of interest or at the invitation of friends and are warm. Most youth leaders will have a group with the full range, even if that's just five young people!

How then do you cater for such a spectrum? It's not easy, but it is possible with the right mindset!

### Depth Versus Accessibility

Imagine being asked at a restaurant, "Would you like milk or solid food this evening?" You'd probably laugh. Anyone outside of infancy is unlikely to request a bottle of milk for their meal at a fine-dining restaurant. But equally, most of us would pass on the grandness of ordering caviar, even if we could afford it.

Yet in our teaching to teens, we often swing between those very extremes. We can end up providing dumbed-down basics (milk) to those who are ready for something chewier, or at the other end of the spectrum, we feed deep-dive theology (caviar) to those who aren't yet able to appreciate it.

This image (more or less) is a biblical one. Those new to the faith are likened to babies:

> *Like newborn babies, crave pure spiritual milk, so that by it you may grow up in your salvation. (1 Peter 2:2)*

But those who are deeper in their faith have different dietary expectations:

> *Anyone who lives on milk, being still an infant, is not acquainted with the teaching about righteousness. But solid food is for the mature, who by constant use have trained themselves to distinguish good from evil.*
>
> *(Hebrews 5:13-14)*

Some need milk, and others need solid food. We don't give steak to toddlers! Similarly, we shouldn't throw deep theology at unchurched young people without context. They can't digest that kind of food yet. But at the same time, it would be wrong to give "milk" to those teens who are ready for "solid food"—those who understand the basics of their faith and are ready to go deeper in their knowledge of God.

Alongside spiritual maturity, we also need to consider educational ability and level of knowledge. You may have a mature Christian in your group who is severely dyslexic, so asking them to read long portions of the Bible and write down their reflections will just stress them out. Or you might have an unchurched young person who loves to think deeply and will come to you with a long, written-out list of questions they want answers to! So it isn't just about complex theological concepts for the mature versus simple ones for those new to Christianity. It's also about accessibility and relevance.

How can we build complexity and accessibility, depth and simplicity into the same session? Here are a few ideas.

### AVOID JARGON

An unchurched teen once asked, "How can I have a relationship with a dead person?" They had heard a speaker invite people to know Jesus but hadn't been told that Jesus had risen again. And the idea of having a "relationship" with someone you can't see or hear just seemed weird. You can understand the confusion!

Phrases like "the blood of the lamb", "Christ's body, broken for you", or "tithes and offerings" mean very little without explanation. They can even be off-putting or misunderstood. Let's do our best to think through what language we're using!

### EXPLAIN

In the book of Acts, an Ethiopian eunuch is struggling to comprehend the biblical text he is reading. Philip, sent by the Holy Spirit, is instructed to start a conversation.

> *Philip ran up to the chariot and heard the man reading Isaiah the prophet. "Do you understand what you are reading?" Philip asked.*
>
> *"How can I," he said, "unless someone explains it to me?" So he invited Philip to come up and sit with him.*
>
> *(Acts 8:30-31)*

What this story so beautifully demonstrates is not the

need to dumb down or change our message but rather the importance of explaining. The eunuch is reading Isaiah—that's not easy! But Philip is able to explain what he is reading and tell him about Jesus.

What do the young people in your setting know already about God and the Bible, and what do they not know? If you're not sure, ask them! The more clarity you can have on this, the better job you can do at explaining things for them in words they can understand.

**BE RELEVANT**

Let's imagine you're teaching on the temple curtain being torn in two when Jesus died. Young people who are mature in their faith can explore themes of access, priesthood and reverence. They know something about how the temple operated in Old Testament times and will see how amazing it is that the curtain was torn. There is a wonderful message for them to grasp about God's holiness, our unworthiness and the grace of Jesus.

You can already see that there is a barrier of language there. Unchurched teens might not know what the word "holy" even means. They need help to understand the concepts you're describing.

But they also need help to understand why these concepts are relevant to them. You need to add hooks that will connect what you're saying with their actual lived experience.

To go back to the temple curtain example, maybe you'll start by talking about broken relationships—the pain of disconnection from a loved one and the relief when a barrier is broken down. Reconciliation with God is like an even more important version of reconciliation with a difficult family member.

Or maybe they need help to understand what a big deal it is to connect with God. You'll talk about trying to visit the king. You can't just go to Buckingham Palace; you need an invitation, the right clothes, and the right behaviour! But with God, through Jesus, the door is always open.

## Setting Two Bars

I would advise you to think in terms of setting two bars. A high bar for depth and maturity (solids) and a low bar for accessibility (milk). Always have both bars in mind. Don't hold back from exploring deep truths, complex passages and big concepts (the high bar). But make sure that it's as jargon-free as possible, properly explained and rooted in everyday life for the teens who are new to it all (the low bar). This way, everyone can engage with the same message at their own level.

When I led a youth group in the Middle East, we had 100 young people attending regularly. We provided food, games, worship, testimonies, Bible study and prayer. We taught from Wayne Grudem's *Systematic Theology*—hardly lightweight stuff. Yet some parents still came to me complaining that it wasn't deep enough!

What I learned was this: it's not about how deep you go; it's about how many on-ramps you offer into that depth. The same room had mature teens grappling with predestination and unchurched kids wondering if they were made for a reason. Both were encountering God because the teaching allowed space for both.

The two-bar system only works if mature believers are present. They not only eat solids but model faith, ask questions and carry the group spiritually. If your group is mostly unchurched or apathetic, then pitch the session primarily for them. Set one bar for now—and grow them into needing two.

One more thought on this: never underestimate peer power. When a young person shares something real—even if it's awkward or unpolished—it often lands harder than your most prepared talk. Use it. Encourage it. But stay ready to teach, guide and frame the moment.

## Build In Balance

I mentioned in chapter 9 how the Bible describes the way Jesus grew during his youth:

> *And Jesus grew in wisdom and stature, and in favour with God and man. (Luke 2:52)*

That covers four types of development: mental, physical, spiritual and social. It's my conviction that we need to think in terms of the same four areas of development for young people today.

That means we don't just do teaching. A youth session built on this framework might include the following:

- Physical: engaging activities or movement
- Mental: Bible teaching that requires processing
- Social: group discussion and relational connection
- Spiritual: opportunities for prayer, reflection or worship

For example, here's an example of how a youth group session on identity might go. See if you can spot what is physical, mental, social and spiritual.

Begin and end the session with hangout time. Provide things for the young people to do together and chat to them about how their week has been.

Start the session proper by playing a game. Place a label on each person's head with the name of a famous person. They must rush around the room asking yes/no questions to each other to discover who is on their label—"Am I a sportsperson?", "Am I American?" and so on. They cannot ask someone twice until they have asked everyone. Finish the game by explaining that today's session will be about our identity.

Have the group sit in a circle, with one person holding a ball. The person with the ball must throw it to someone else and say something positive about that person. Then the person who now has the ball must do the same. Give them time to think, but once you're in the flow, speed it up and go several rounds. Finally, ask the group, "What did it feel like to throw the ball and have to think of something to say?" and then "When you caught the ball and someone said something about you, how did that make you feel?" Finish by saying that when people speak things over us, we connect it to our identity—who we are.

Now you are ready to explore the Bible with the young people. Try reading a passage aloud and tell the group that they need to listen because they are going to go into groups and discuss what they've heard. Give them Bibles so that they can look up the reference for themselves.

Let's imagine you start by focusing on 1 Samuel 16:7—"People look at the outward appearance, but the LORD looks at the heart". You might want to explain the context or read a longer passage, depending on the group.

Before placing the young people in groups, ensure each group has either a leader or a mature young person who can help the others where there is varied understanding.

Give them two or three questions to discuss:

- Is there a difference between our outward appearance and who we are inside?
- What about the difference between who we are in our hearts and what we do in practice? Do you think the two are linked?
- Is it good news or bad news that God looks at the heart? Why do you think that?

Once you have given them some time to discuss, take feedback.

You could carry on by exploring other passages of Scripture or by sharing some thoughts on what Jesus thinks about us and what he wants for our lives. Talk about your own journey and your own life to help the young people think about how this could apply to theirs.

As you close, invite the group into a moment of prayer. You could ask them to close their eyes and imagine that they are standing looking at God. What would he say about them? Ask them to imagine him saying their name and telling them how much he loves them and wants them to know him. Close by praying aloud and thank everyone for coming.

You may ask why it's important to consider things like games and relational time. Don't young people get that elsewhere? Well, throughout this book I've been building the case that we need to care for the whole person. It isn't just about hitting young people with a five-minute gospel presentation and hoping they convert. We have so much more to offer them than that! Remember earlier on in the book when we talked about how the church offers a place to belong, to feel like family, to connect intergenerationally and to create safety and security? All of those things are formed from relational currency and building a healthy and appropriate bond.

## A Church That Welcomes

Here's the really good news: one in three young people want someone to share their faith with them.[75] Even more would consider going to church if a friend invited them. In fact, 60% of young people are either open or warm to the idea of church.

So why don't more young people in churches invite their friends? Two reasons: fear of rejection and fear of what their friends will experience if they come.

At one session, Ella, age 13, shared that her friends wouldn't come because they believed the church hated gay and trans people. Even though her church doesn't hate anyone and holds a posture of grace, her friends had a different perception.

That perception is powerful, even if it's not rooted in personal experience. Many young people are hesitant to engage with anything seen as intolerant, even if they aren't directly affected. Still, the majority of unchurched young people are either indifferent or open, not hostile—especially if they trust their Christian friends. Seven out of ten believe they'd feel welcome if they visited.

We can't change everyone's perception instantly, but we can work on creating spaces that feel welcoming, loving and open—without compromising truth.

### Taste and See

Psalm 34:8 says, "Taste and see that the LORD is good". The invitation is just to try it! That's our goal in youth ministry—to create a space where anyone can take a seat at the table, find something nourishing, and leave feeling drawn closer to Jesus.

A youth ministry that holds milk and solids at the same table, that builds in balance and that believes young people are not only welcome but essential to the church's future—that's a youth ministry worth shaping. That's a youth ministry that will grow and attract the unchurched and churched, the seeker and those who have already found Jesus. That's my prayer for you and your ministry.

Conclusion

# Now What?

**MOVING FROM VISION** to conviction and determining direction is exciting and energising. If you can picture what something might look like and have a dream of the desired outcome, that is a beautiful moment! I'm hoping that you have experienced a moment like that as you have read this book: that you have shared it with others and prayed through its contents. Or perhaps you are still processing and seeking God's will—that's fine too.

Throughout the book, I've tried to help you see the world through the lens of Gen Z-A. I'm hoping you have a clearer understanding of who they are, what they care about and what they are facing. I'm also hoping you have a sense of conviction and excitement bubbling up about what you could do to reach out and welcome young people who right now have no idea that there is life on offer in Jesus.

But now comes the challenging part: making it happen! God is moving, and unchurched young people are responding, but many don't know entirely what they're experiencing or how to act on what they sense. By asking God to be at work in your setting and making yourself available, you will join this incredible wave of the Spirit and, hopefully, get to connect young people's seeking with the one who pursues them every day of their lives.

### Power in Weakness

Experience tells me that even if the research has persuaded you, and the stories and arguments about how we need to engage with young people are compelling, there is still a chance you won't move to action. Somewhere in the depths of your subconscious may be an unspoken belief that you can't do it! In other churches perhaps they can, but in your church isn't it just wishful thinking?

I sympathise. As experienced as I might appear on paper and in years of youth work, I very often feel inadequate—not necessarily from poor self-confidence but rather because of the scale and importance of the mission. But here is what I really know: if God has called us, then we should not despise the small beginnings (Zechariah 4:10). He loves our obedience and faithfulness. Let me tell you about Sarah.

All Sarah had was a toaster and a couple of volunteers. That's all she needed to approach the principal of one of the largest schools in the area. At their first meeting, Sarah was almost immediately dismissed: "Whatever you would like to do in this school, I can't let you. Behaviour here is so bad that visitors really get a tough time, and the pupils don't calm down for the rest of the day." But Sarah was not dismayed. She simply asked, "Can I run a breakfast club? I would like to feed anyone who hasn't had breakfast. All I can offer is toast, but might that be helpful?"

The principal had not expected this. She reluctantly said yes. By the end of the first week, Sarah was providing toast for almost the entire school. (That's a lot of toast!) She was reaching hundreds of pupils every day. By the end of the second week, the school principal was asking, "What else can you do? The pupils' behaviour has changed remarkably in the last two weeks!"

All it took was toast, and Sarah now has an open door to do so much more, with the school providing support to help her. It started with the only thing she had: a toaster. Sarah went from physically feeding young people to being able to spiritually feed them, as the principal allowed her to run a Christian club at lunchtime. Who said you need to be the biggest or the best to make an impact?

For me, it all comes down to a simple question: why are you interested in helping out? Suppose it's to meet your own needs. In that case, politely, I might suggest you find something else to do. If it's to gain experience and climb the ministry ladder, maybe find another way of doing that. But if it's to help a young person discover Jesus and see their lives changed by him, then God has more than enough to work with. It is often said that youth work is the one area of church ministry where you never really know your impact over the long haul. That is true—but as you develop relationships, you will see enough change to know you are making a difference. Remember the story of my trip up Kilimanjaro? Go slow, and go together. The summit awaits.

# Forming a Plan

Here are some questions to help you develop a clear plan with tangible actions.

### Setting the Vision

Why do young people outside the church matter to you?

What do you long to see God do in their lives?

What do you sense God is asking you to do?

**Developing a Plan**

Where will you do it?

What do you need in order to do it?

Who do you need?

**Gathering Resources**

What resources do you already have?

What can you easily get by asking others in the church?

What else do you need?

Who could you ask for help or advice to get these resources?

## Starting with Prayer

When will you meet to pray about your plan?

Who will you meet with?

How will you pray?

## Getting Going

What is your first step?

What is your second step?

What is your third step?

# Acknowledgements

I am and always will be profoundly grateful to Youth for Christ. Its influence upon me cannot be understated. It was through its mission that I came to faith at the age of 16, was trained, found my wife Joy and then served for 34 years locally, nationally and internationally. My children were born and raised on the mission field and travelled the world with me and Joy as I served. Just before this book went to print, I stepped down as the National Director of British Youth for Christ to embark on something new outside of this incredible ministry. But the heartbeat of Youth for Christ—to see young people's lives changed by Jesus and support the local church in that task—will forever stir within me.

There are many names I could and should acknowledge, but the tribute would be longer than the book itself! However, one person who created the backdrop to much of this book is Laura Hancock, who led all of the research within British Youth for Christ over my tenure and helped us to gain strategic clarity regarding young people, the church and sharing the gospel. This book is built upon the insights and trends of that research, as well as on the experience of the hundreds of staff who serve every day.

The other person I must mention is Katy Morgan, who took my jumbled thoughts and helped to make sense of them as she edited this book.

Ultimately I thank God for the move of his Spirit in our current time, with many unchurched young people seeking Jesus and looking to the church for answers.

# Notes


1 Peter Brierley, *UK Church Statistics, No. 2, 2010 to 2020* (ADBC Publishers, 2014).

2 *Z-A: Growing Spirituality* (British Youth for Christ / DJS Research, 2025), p. 38-43.

3 *Z-A: Growing Spirituality* (British Youth for Christ / DJS Research, 2025), p. 38-43.

4 Rhiannon McAleer and Rob Barward-Symmons, *The Quiet Revival* (Bible Society, 2025), p. 16.

5 These may not be Smith's exact words. You will find slightly different versions of this quote in a variety of places.

6 "Gen Z and Service Attendance: Why They Don't Go (More Often)" (Springtide Research Institute, 15 Feb. 2024): springtideresearch.org/post/religion-and-spirituality/gen-z-and-service-attendance-why-they-dont-go-more-often (accessed 25 Jul. 2025).

7 Olivia Petter, "WitchTok: How witchcraft became the latest controversial wellness fad" (*The Independent*, 27 Jul. 2024): www.independent.co.uk/life-style/witchcraft-wellness-witchtok-kate-tomas-b2585162.html (accessed 25 Jul. 2025).

8 Mel Lacy, "The Allure and Danger of WitchTok: Guiding the Next Generation Toward Biblical Truth" (Growing Young Disciples, 9 Sep. 2024): www.growingyoungdisciples.co.uk/the-allure-and-danger-of-witchtok-guiding-the-next-generation-toward-biblical-truth (accessed 25 Jul. 2025).

9 "Religion and Spirituality among Teens and Young Adults:

Identity and Belief" (Springtide Research Institute, 21 Jan. 2025): springtideresearch.org/post/religion-and-spirituality/identity-and-belief (accessed 25 Jul. 2025).

10 Lauren Moss and Elaine Dunkley, "Pupil behaviour 'getting worse' at schools in England, say teachers" (*BBC News*, 28 Mar. 2024): www.bbc.co.uk/news/education-68674568 (accessed 25 Jul. 2025).

11 Halima Jibril, "What is going on with Gen Alpha boys?" (*Dazed*, 6 Apr. 2024): www.dazeddigital.com/life-culture/article/62302/1/what-is-really-going-on-with-gen-alpha-boys-andrew-tate-misogyny (accessed 22 Jan. 2025).

12 Will Vernon, "Suicide is on the rise for young Americans, with no clear answers" (*BBC News*, 11 Apr. 2024): www.bbc.co.uk/news/world-us-canada-68782177 (accessed 25 Jul. 2025).

13 Shannon Brown, "Children as young as 13 sold knives and blades in police sting operation" (*Bristol Live*, 23 Apr. 2024): www.bristolpost.co.uk/news/bristol-news/children-young-13-sold-knives-9242736 (accessed 25 Jul. 2025).

14 Catriona Aitken, Peter Shuttleworth and Oliver Slow, "Arrest and three hurt amid reports of school stabbing" (*BBC News*, 24 Apr. 2024): www.bbc.co.uk/news/live/uk-wales-68890153 (accessed 25 Jul. 2025).

15 Philippa Roxby and Elena Bailey, "England child alcohol use tops global chart, finds WHO report" (*BBC News*, 25 Apr. 2024): www.bbc.co.uk/news/health-68884005 (accessed 25 Jul. 2025).

16 *Z-A: Growing Spirituality* (British Youth for Christ / DJS Research, 2025), p. 36.

17 *Gen Z: Rethinking Culture* (British Youth for Christ / DJS Research, 2017), and *Z-A of Faith and Spirituality* (British Youth for Christ / DJS Research, 2020), p. 13.

18 Dr Sarah Jenkins, Isabella Pereira and Natalie Evans, *Families in Britain* (Ipsos MORI, 2009), p. 12: www.policyexchange.org.

uk/wp-content/uploads/2016/09/families-in-britain-apr-09.pdf (accessed 25 Jul. 2025).

19 "Families and Households in the UK: 2024" (Office for National Statistics, 23 Jul. 2025).

20 "Children in families in England and Wales: Census 2021" (Office for National Statistics, 5 Mar. 2024).

21 Linda J. Waite and Maggie Gallagher, *The Case for Marriage* (Crown, 2001).

22 Juan Carlos Martín Quintana, Pedro Francisco Alemán Ramos and Paula Morales Almeida, "The Influence of Perceived Security in Childhood on Adult Self-Concept: The Mediating Role of Resilience and Self-Esteem", *Healthcare*, vol. 11 (17) (2023), p. 2435: doi.org/10.3390/healthcare11172435 (accessed 15 Aug. 2025).

23 Rhiannon McAleer and Rob Barward-Symmons, *The Quiet Revival* (Bible Society 2025), p. 34, 37.

24 Pravina Rudra, "Is Gen Z the most conservative generation in history?" (*The New Statesman*, 28 Nov. 2023): www.newstatesman.com/politics/society/2023/11/gen-z-most-conservative-generation-radical-youth (accessed 25 Jul. 2025).

25 Robert Booth and Michael Goodier, "Young people in England and Wales twice as likely to identify as LGB+" (*The Guardian*, 25 Jan. 2023): www.theguardian.com/society/2023/jan/25/young-people-england-wales-twice-likely-identify-lgb-overall-population (accessed 25 Jul. 2025).

26 Pravina Rudra, "Is Gen Z the most conservative generation in history?" (*The New Statesman*, 28 Nov. 2023) (see note 24).

27 Jessica Klein, "How some young people are shaking off gender binaries" (*BBC Worklife*, 29 Mar. 2023): www.bbc.co.uk/worklife/article/20230327-how-young-people-are-shaking-off-gender-binaries (accessed 25 Jul. 2025).

28 Luke Tryl, Tyron Surmon, Arisa Kimaram and Conleth Burns, *Britons and Gender Identity: Navigating Common Ground and*

*Division* (More in Common, 2022), p. 19.

29 For example, try *Why Does God Care Who I Sleep With?* by Sam Allberry or *Does the Bible Affirm Same-Sex Relationships?* by Rebecca McLaughlin.

30 www.samaritans.org/about-samaritans/research-policy/young-people-suicide (accessed 15 Aug. 2025).

31 Aric Sigman, "Time for a view on screen time", *Archives of Disease in Childhood*, vol. 97 (11) (2012), p. 935: www.researchgate.net/publication/232222451_Time_for_a_view_on_screen_time (accessed 15 Aug. 2025).

32 Ellyn Briggs, "Gen Alpha Is in Its Tablet Era" (Morning Consult, 8 Mar. 2024): pro.morningconsult.com/analysis/gen-alpha-device-ownership-tablets-smartphones-2024 (accessed 15 Aug. 2025).

33 "30+ Average Screen Time Statistics for 2024" (SlickText, 6 Mar. 2025): www.slicktext.com/blog/2023/01/30-key-screen-time-statistics-for-2022-2023 (accessed 15 Aug. 2025).

34 Fabio Duarte, "Alarming Average Screen Time Statistics" (Exploding Topics, 24 Apr. 2025): explodingtopics.com/blog/screen-time-stats (accessed 15 Aug. 2025).

35 Rebecca Joy Stanborough, "What's Blue Light, and How Does It Affect Our Eyes?" (Healthline, 24 Apr. 2023): www.healthline.com/health/what-is-blue-light (accessed 15 Aug. 2025).

36 Anne-Marie Chang, Daniel Aeschbach, Jean F. Duffy and Charles A. Czeisler, "Evening use of light-emitting eReaders negatively affects sleep, circadian timing, and next-morning alertness", *Proceedings of the National Academy of Sciences*, vol. 112 (4) (2014), p. 1232–1237: doi.org/10.1073/pnas.1418490112 (accessed 15 Aug. 2025).

37 Eric Suni, "Technology in the Bedroom" (Sleep Foundation, 11 Jul. 2025): www.sleepfoundation.org/bedroom-environment/technology-in-the-bedroom (accessed 25 Jul. 2025).

38 Ian Taylor, "How to finally break free from your smartphone addiction" (*BBC Science Focus*, 4 Feb. 2024): www.sciencefocus.

com/science/dopamine-fasting-smartphone-addiction (accessed 15 Aug. 2025).

39 "Dealing with Devices: The Parent-Teen Dynamic" (Common Sense Media): www.commonsensemedia.org/technology-addiction-concern-controversy-and-finding-balance-infographic (accessed 15 Aug. 2025).

40 Camilla Foster, "Screen time rewires your child's brain – here's what you can do about it" (*The Independent*, 1 May 2025): www.independent.co.uk/life-style/health-and-families/screen-time-children-effects-brain-b2748737.html (accessed 25 Jul. 2025).

41 Kevin McSpadden, "You now have a shorter attention span than a goldfish" (*Time*, 14 May 2015): time.com/3858309/attention-spans-goldfish (accessed 25 Jul. 2025).

42 Stuart Wolpert, "Is technology producing a decline in critical thinking and analysis?" (*UCLA Newsroom*, 27 Jan. 2009): newsroom.ucla.edu/releases/is-technology-producing-a-decline-79127 (accessed 25 Jul. 2025).

43 Adrian F. Ward, Kristen Duke, Ayelet Gneezy, and Maarten W. Bos, "Brain Drain: The Mere Presence of One's Own Smartphone Reduces Available Cognitive Capacity", *Journal of the Association for Consumer Research*, vol. 2 (2) (2017), p. 140–154: ddoi.org/10.1086/691462 (accessed 15 Aug. 2025).

44 "Razorfish Study Unveils Generation Alpha Insights, Preparing Brands for the Next Consumer Cohort" (Razorfish, 1 Aug. 2023): www.razorfish.com/articles/news/razorfish-study-unveils-generation-alpha-insights (accessed 15 Aug. 2025).

45 Lauren Edwards, "Gen Z say lack of internet access should be treated as human rights issue" (*Daily Mirror*, 21 Feb. 2025): www.mirror.co.uk/tech/gen-z-say-lack-internet-34724148 (accessed 25 Jul. 2025).

46 *Children and Parents: Media Use and Attitudes* (Ofcom 2023), p. 9: www.ofcom.org.uk/siteassets/resources/documents/research-

and-data/media-literacy-research/children/childrens-media-use-and-attitudes-2023/childrens-media-use-and-attitudes-report-2023.pdf (accessed 15 Aug. 2025).

47 Jean M. Twenge, "Have Smartphones Destroyed a Generation?" (*The Atlantic*, Sep. 2017): www.theatlantic.com/magazine/archive/2017/09/has-the-smartphone-destroyed-a-generation/534198 (accessed 13 Aug. 2025).

48 "What young people really think about social media" (The Children's Society, 18 May 2021): www.childrenssociety.org.uk/what-we-do/blogs/what-young-people-think-about-social-media (accessed 25 Jul. 2025).

49 www.nspcc.org.uk/keeping-children-safe/online-safety/social-media (accessed 13 Aug. 2025).

50 "ESET UK Research reveals teenage sexting epidemic – with almost three-quarters of U18s regretting sharing intimate photos and videos online" (ESET, 12 Feb. 2024): www.eset.com/uk/about/newsroom/press-releases/eset-uk-think-twice-sexting-epidemic (accessed 15 Aug. 2025).

51 Thomas Kingsley, "One in five 13-14-year-olds have seen drugs being sold on social media" (*The Independent*, 3 Nov. 2021): www.independent.co.uk/news/uk/drugs-young-people-social-media-b1949196.html (accessed 15 Aug. 2025).

52 Dan Milmo and Alex Hern, "TikTok self-harm study results 'every parent's nightmare'" (*The Guardian*, 15 Dec. 2022): www.theguardian.com/technology/2022/dec/15/tiktok-self-harm-study-results-every-parents-nightmare (accessed 28 Aug. 2025).

53 Sarah Marsh, "About 7% of UK children have attempted suicide by age of 17 – study" (*The Guardian*, 21 Feb. 2021): www.theguardian.com/society/2021/feb/21/uk-17-year-olds-mental-health-crisis (accessed 15 Aug. 2025).

54 Cambridge Dictionary: cambridge.org/dictionary/english/cancel-culture (accessed 25 Jul. 2025).

55 Robert Booth, "'It's out of order': Gen Z speak up for cancel culture and 'young illiberal progressives'" (*The Guardian*, 1 Nov. 2022): www.theguardian.com/society/2022/nov/01/its-out-of-order-gen-z-speak-up-on-cancel-culture-and-young-illiberal-progressives (accessed 25 Jul. 2025).

56 Sanam Yar and Jonah E. Bromwich, "Tales From the Teenage Cancel Culture" (*The New York Times*, 31 Oct, 2019): www.nytimes.com/2019/10/31/style/cancel-culture.html (accessed 25 Jul. 2025).

57 "How Counselors Are Dealing With The Impact Of Cancel Culture On Mental Health (Carlow University, 8 Dec. 2022): carlow.blogs.elliance.com/2022/12/08/how-counselors-are-dealing-with-an-impact-of-cancel-culture-on-mental-health (accessed 25 Jul. 2025).

58 Ethan Kross, Marc G. Berman, Walter Mischel, Edward E. Smith and Tor D. Wager, "Social Rejection Shares Somatosensory Representations with Physical Pain", *Proceedings of the National Academy of Sciences*, vol. 108 (15) (2011), p.6270–6275: doi.org/10.1073/pnas.1102693108 (accessed 25 Jul. 2025).

59 Lindsey Toler, "The Mental Health Effects of Cancel Culture" (Verywell Mind, 30 Jul. 2025): www.verywellmind.com/the-mental-health-effects-of-cancel-culture-5119201 (accessed 15 Aug. 2025).

60 "Mental health pressures in England" (The British Medical Association, 17 Jul. 2025): www.bma.org.uk/advice-and-support/nhs-delivery-and-workforce/pressures/mental-health-pressures-data-analysis (accessed 13 Aug. 2025).

61 "Mental Health of Children and Young People in England, 2023" (NHS, 21 Nov. 2023): digital.nhs.uk/data-and-information/publications/statistical/mental-health-of-children-and-young-people-in-england/2023-wave-4-follow-up (accessed 13 Aug. 2025).

62 Zara Abrams, "Kids' mental health is in crisis. Here's what psychologists are doing to help", *American Psychological Association, 2023 Trends Report* (1 Jan. 2023): www.apa.org/monitor/2023/01/

trends-improving-youth-mental-health (accessed 15 Aug. 2025).

63 Peter Gray, David F. Lancy and David F. Bjorklund, "Decline in Independent Activity as a Cause of Decline in Children's Mental Wellbeing: Summary of the Evidence", *The Journal of Pediatrics* vol. 260 (2) (2023): www.researchgate.net/publication/368794518_Decline_in_Independent_Activity_as_a_Cause_of_Decline_in_Children (accessed 15 Aug. 2025).

64 Rhiannon McAleer and Rob Barward-Symmons, *The Quiet Revival* (Bible Society 2025), p. 24.

65 *Gen Z: Rethinking Culture* (British Youth for Christ / DJS Research, 2017).

66 *Z-A: Growing Spirituality* (British Youth for Christ / DJS Research, 2025), p. 10. The young people were allowed to give multiple answers.

67 *Youth provision and life outcomes* (SQW, 2024), p. 31: assets.publishing.service.gov.uk/media/65ce41c3423931001bb7b8b7/Local_Areas_-_Report_-_Youth_Evidence_Base-accessible.pdf (accessed 15 Aug. 2025).

68 *School Standards and Framework Act 1998, Chapter 31* (The Stationery Office Limited, 1998), section 6: www.legislation.gov.uk/ukpga/1998/31/pdfs/ukpga_19980031_en.pdf (accessed 13 Aug. 2025).

69 Department for Education, "Religious Education and Collective Worship", Circular number 1/94: assets.publishing.service.gov.uk/media/5a7cd8f740f0b6629523c2b7/Collective_worship_in_schools.pdf (accessed 13 Aug. 2025).

70 *The Annual Report of His Majesty's Chief Inspector of Education, Children's Services and Skills 2022/23* (Crown copyright, 2023): www.gov.uk/government/publications/ofsted-annual-report-202223-education-childrens-services-and-skills/the-annual-report-of-his-majestys-chief-inspector-of-education-childrens-services-and-skills-202223 (accessed 14 Aug. 2025).

71 "Most Churches Have Less Than Five Young People" (*The Church of England Newspaper*, 6 Jun. 2019): www.churchnewspaper.com/most-churches-have-less-than-five-young-people (accessed 25 Jul. 2025).

72 *Youth and Children Growth Research* (Church of England, 2022), p. 2: www.churchofengland.org/sites/default/files/2022-07/youth-and-childrens-growth-research-paper.pdf (accessed 25 Jul. 2025).

73 Peter Brierley, *UK Church Statistics, No. 2, 2010 to 2020* (ADBC Publishers, 2014).

74 *Z-A: Growing Spirituality* (British Youth for Christ / DJS Research, 2025), p. 37.

75 *Z-A: Growing Spirituality* (British Youth for Christ / DJS Research, 2025) p. 23.

YOUTH FOR CHRIST

This book is part of the wider efforts of British Youth for Christ to equip and train local churches to reach out to unchurched young people with the gospel.

To find out more, go to yfc.co.uk.